TOP **10**
VANCOUVER
&VICTORIA

CONSTANCE BRISSENDEN

DK
EYEWITNESS TRAVEL

Left **False Creek, Vancouver** Right **Storefront, Robson Street**

LONDON, NEW YORK,
MELBOURNE, MUNICH AND DELHI
www.dk.com

Produced by
International Book Productions Inc., Toronto

Printed and bound by South China Printing
Co. Ltd., China

First American Edition, 2006
14 15 16 17 10 9 8 7 6 5 4 3 2 1

Published in the United States by
DK Publishing, 345 Hudson Street,
New York, New York 10014

Reprinted with revisions 2008, 2010,
2012, 2014

**Copyright 2006, 2014 © Dorling
Kindersley Limited**

All rights reserved. Without limiting the rights under
copyright reserved above, no part of this publication
may be reproduced, stored in or introduced into a
retrieval system, or transmitted, in any form, or by
any means (electronic, mechanical, photocopying,
recording, or otherwise), without prior written
permission of both the copyright owner and the
above publisher of this book. Published in Great
Britain by Dorling Kindersley Limited.

A cataloging in publication record is available from
the Library of Congress.

ISSN 1479-344X
ISBN 978-1-46540-997-3

Within each Top 10 list in this book, no hierarchy of quality or
popularity is implied. All 10 are, in the editor's opinion, of
roughly equal merit.

Floors are referred to in accordance with American usage, ie
the "first floor" is at ground level.

MIX
Paper from
responsible sources
FSC
www.fsc.org   FSC™ C018179

Contents

Vancouver & Victoria's Top 10

**The information in this DK Eyewitness Top 10 Travel Guide
is checked regularly.**

Every effort has been made to ensure that this book is as up-to-date as possible at the time of
going to press. Some details, however, such as telephone numbers, opening hours, prices,
gallery hanging arrangements and travel information are liable to change. The publishers
cannot accept responsibility for any consequences arising from the use of this book, nor for
any material on third party websites, and cannot guarantee that any website address in this
book will be a suitable source of travel information. We value the views and suggestions of
our readers very highly. Please write to: Publisher, DK Eyewitness Travel Guides,
Dorling Kindersley, 80 Strand, London, WC2R 0RL, UK, or email: travelguides@dk.com.

Cover: Front – **Dorling Kindersley**: Rough Guides/Tim Draper bl; **age fotostock**: David Nunuk main. Spine
– **Dorling Kindersley**: Gunter Marx b. Back – **Dorling Kindersley**: Gunter Marx c, cl, cr. Front Flap – Royal
British Columbia Museum crb.

Key to abbreviations
Adm admission charge payable

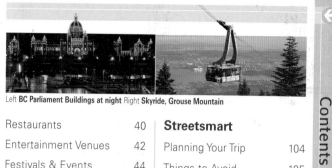
Left **BC Parliament Buildings at night** Right **Skyride, Grouse Mountain**

Left **Totem Poles, Stanley Park** Right **Skier, Whistler Mountain**

Following pages **Aerial view of downtown Vancouver with Canada Place in the foreground**

VANCOUVER AND VICTORIA'S TOP 10

VANCOUVER & VICTORIA'S TOP 10

TOP 10 Vancouver & Victoria Highlights

Fringed by the Pacific Ocean's sandy beaches, with a backdrop of the Coast Mountain range, Vancouver is among the most beautifully located metropolises on earth. Also feted as the world's most livable city, this West Coast gem has a lively cultural scene and superb restaurants and hotels. On Vancouver Island, a short ferry ride away, Victoria offers visitors a unique blend of old-world charm and new-world experiences. The city is an excellent starting-off point from which to explore the many natural wonders of the island.

Stanley Park
Created in 1886, Stanley Park is North America's third-largest urban park. It juts into Burrard Inlet, offering an enticing combination of forest, ocean, and beaches, and an encircling seawall pedestrian loop *(see pp8–11)*.

Canada Place
Built for Expo '86, Canada Place is now an outstanding convention and hotel complex overlooking Vancouver Harbour. Cruise ships dock alongside an inviting promenade *(see pp12–13)*.

Capilano Suspension Bridge Park
Teetering over a wooden bridge high above the Capilano River is perhaps the most thrilling experience here; walking along a boardwalk into the treetops a close second. Learn about local history, forest ecology, and First Nations culture as you enjoy the surroundings *(see pp14–15)*.

UBC Museum of Anthropology
In a stunning building, overlooking mountains and sea, is one of North America's finest collections of Northwest Coast native art. The museum's Koerner Ceramics Gallery houses 15th- to 19th-century European ceramics *(see pp16–17)*.

Vancouver Art Gallery
From the swirling raincoast forests of famed BC artist Emily Carr to radical conceptual installations, the gallery features the best of West Coast and international art *(see pp18–19)*.

Devonian Harbour Park

Stanley Park 1

WEST GEORGIA STREET

DENMAN STREET

ROBSON

West End

Alexandra Park

DAVIE STREET

BEACH AVENUE

Nelson P

English Bay 4

Vanier Park

PACIFIC STREET

BURRARD STREET

GRANVILLE STREET

6 Granville Island

Sutcliffe Park

Science World
Science comes alive inside the dome-shaped Science World. Hands-on exhibits capture the imaginations of all ages, with fresh approaches to science in all its dimensions *(see pp22–3)*.

Granville Island
The popular island on False Creek is a bustling mix of shops, galleries, restaurants, and theaters – fun both to visit and explore *(see pp20–21)*.

Royal British Columbia Museum
A wonderful museum, confidently portraying BC's history and natural assets in creative galleries *(see pp24–5)*.

Long Beach Area
Spectacular scenery dominates the Long Beach area on Vancouver Island's West Coast. Wild Pacific shores and rare old-growth forests make the region the perfect destination to experience the essence of rugged BC *(see pp26–7)*.

Whistler
Ideal for a day-trip or a longer visit, Whistler is an upscale resort town a two-hour drive north from Vancouver. Two mountains tower over alpine-style resort villages. Skiers abound here but countless other year-round activities ensure Whistler has something for everyone *(see pp28–31)*.

🔟 Stanley Park

A local favorite since the Victorian era, spectacular Stanley Park is a mere 10-minute bus ride from downtown. Forest walks, beachside strolls, and a vibrant rose garden are among its natural attractions. Amusing activities include a popular children's waterpark and farmyard, tennis courts, and a pitch-and-putt course. Located in the park, the Vancouver Aquarium Marine Science Centre (see pp10–11) is world-renowned for its realistic walk-through exhibits based on scientific research projects.

Inukshuk, English Bay

🍴 Four fine-dining restaurants and many refreshment kiosks offer plenty of food options. The Fish House in Stanley Park serves afternoon tea. UpStream Café in the aquarium has coffees and sandwiches.

🚗 Traffic in the park is one way, counterclockwise. Pay parking is strictly enforced.

Bicycle & in-line skate rentals: 604 688 2453.

- Map G1
- 311
- www.vancouver parks.ca
- Open 24 hrs daily (not all sights)
- Adm to some activities
- Vancouver Aquarium: 845 Avison Way, 604 659 3474, www.vanaqua.org; Open late Jun–Aug: 9:30am–7pm; Sep–mid-Jun: 10am–5pm; Adm: Adult $21; Seniors, youths & students $16; Children $13 (under 3s free)

Top 10 Features

1. English Bay
2. Siwash Rock
3. Beaver Lake
4. Seawall
5. Lost Lagoon
6. Brockton Point
7. Brockton Point Visitor Centre
8. Vancouver Aquarium
9. Prospect Point
10. Rose Garden

English Bay
The sandy beaches draw crowds to enjoy strolls and the view. The heated saltwater pool at Second Beach offers a warmer alternative to the bay. Kids delight in the play area nearby. Sunbathers relax against driftwood logs at Third Beach.

Siwash Rock
According to Squamish legend, this ancient lava rock deposit (above) jutting up from the water was once an Indian warrior, turned to stone.

Beaver Lake
Hiking trails to Beaver Lake through a raincoast forest follow old logging roads. Frogs, raccoons, rabbits, and even coyote may be spotted at the natural-state lake fringed by cattails and water lilies.

Seawall
Pedestrians, cyclists, and in-line skaters happily share the 6-miles (10-km) paved path ringing the park (center), with its unimpeded views of English Bay and Burrard Inlet. Look for unusual features, such as the sculpture Girl in a Wetsuit on an offshore rock.

Lost Lagoon
This willow-fringed lagoon is an inner city wildlife sanctuary, protecting a bevy of wood ducks, blue herons, and white swans. At night, the central fountain is colorfully lit up.

➤ *A delightful 15-minute ride on the miniature railway takes you through a towering West Coast forest*

Brockton Point

The point offers a terrific view of Burrard Inlet. In 1915, a lighthouse *(above)* was built to guide vessels into the harbor. Sailors set their chronometers by the Nine-O'Clock Gun at nearby Hallelujah Point. Its boom has been heard nightly since 1894.

Brockton Point Visitor Centre

Three carved gateways and a cedar-wood interpretive pavilion welcome visitors to the park. One of the poles on display is by Haida artist Bill Reid, who carved a replica of a pre-1878 Skedans mortuary pole *(above)*.

Vancouver Aquarium

Marine displays capture the drama of the West Coast. Five Beluga whales share the space with 70,000 other inhabitants *(see pp10–11)*.

Prospect Point

The view from here, the park's highest point, across the dark blue water of Burrard Inlet to the Coast Mountains is one of the best in the city.

Rose Garden

A formal rose garden *(below)* blossoms year-round. From April to September, a variety of perennial plantings ensure vibrant color.

Chief Joe Capilano

Few knew Stanley Park like Squamish chief Joe Capilano. Born in 1840, Capilano often visited the park, home to some members of his nation. In 1906, he traveled to England to present a petition on Indian rights to King Edward VII. He shared local stories with Mohawk writer Pauline Johnson, who published them in *Legends of Vancouver* in 1911, a year after Capilano died.

Left **Clownfish Cove** Right **Sharks in the Tropic Zone Gallery**

TOP 10 Vancouver Aquarium

1 Wild Coast
Walkways lead past marine creatures from the wild BC West Coast. The animals include frolicking sea otters, playful dolphins, harbor seals, and porpoises as well as African penguins and the often vocal Steller sea lions that are members of a shrinking worldwide population. There are touch-pools with shoreline animals, demonstrations by intepretive staff, and training sessions with marine mammals.

2 Canada's Arctic Habitat
Beluga whales are the main draw here. Visitors admire them from both inside and outside locations. Indoors, on the lower level, two floor-to-ceiling windows allow underwater viewing. Interactive exhibits provide information about the beluga's native arctic environment. For an extra fee, try a Beluga Encounter *(see p11)*.

Sea lion, Wild Coast exhibit

3 Pacific Canada Exhibit
This two-story gallery highlights marine life from the Strait of Georgia and brings visitors face to face with an underwater habitat filled with a vast web of plant and animal life. Divers mingle with thousands of schooling herring, salmon, crabs, kelp, sea stars, and other Pacific marine life. Sturgeon, wolf-eels, and anemones also inhabit this exciting exhibit.

4 Amazon Rainforest
Caimans, members of the crocodilian group, co-exist in a hot, humid jungle setting with well-camouflaged sloths and colorful butterflies that flutter around. Visitors can experience a tropical rainstorm every hour in this exotic space.

5 Clownfish Cove
This interactive play zone, designed to appeal to children eight years of age and younger, features animals such as seahorses, horseshoe crabs, toads, and, of course, clownfish. A make-believe marine mammal rescue hospital allows kids to nurse a toy sick or injured seal pup. Puzzles, puppets, dress-up costumes, and crafts are on hand to amuse the little ones.

6 Tropic Zone Gallery
This gallery highlights the animals found in the tropical reefs of the Indo-Pacific. Learn about the blacktip reef sharks, seahorses, clown anemonefish, and the freshwater species that also call the tropics home.

7 Treasures of the British Columbia Coast
Local waters are the focus of this colorful gallery. Wolf eels, rockfishes, and a giant Pacific octopus can be spied lurking in the depths.

The Vancouver Aquarium was one of the first ever to introduce trained naturalists as guides

Top 10 Historical Highlights

1. The Stanley Park peninsula is inhabited by the Squamish until 1888
2. Deadman's Island, an Indian burial site, visited by first white settler, 1862
3. City council petitions for a permanent park, 1886
4. Governor General Stanley dedicates the park, 1889
5. Nine O'Clock Gun arrives, 1894 *(see p9)*
6. The Hollow Tree, a red cedar 65 ft (20 m) in circumference, is the park's most-photographed attraction, early 1900s
7. Lumberman's Arch is built as a tribute to BC's logging industry, 1912
8. Construction of the seawall begins, to prevent erosion, 1917
9. Lost Lagoon is created by construction of the causeway, early 1920s
10. Guinness family builds Lions Gate Bridge at the park's north end, 1938

History of Stanley Park

Coal Harbour peninsula was inhabited for thousands of years by Musqueam, Tsleil-Waututh, and Squamish Coast Salish nations in a village known as Khwaykhway (pronounced Whoi-whoi). In 1862, the peninsula became a military reserve to protect the harbor from American invasion, but the village and its dwellers were left undisturbed. Stanley Park was established on the former military reserve after the Great Fire of June 13, 1886, destroyed the entire city. The park opened in 1888, and was dedicated by Lord Stanley the following year. By 1892, there was no sign of life left in Khwaykhway – most of the Natives had died in a smallpox epidemic between 1888 and 1892.

Entering Stanley Park

Stanley Park's original entrance was through an arch and over a bridge spanning Coal Harbour.

Beluga Encounters

8 Join a trainer or animal-care specialist behind the scenes and learn about the amazing aquarium animals during a hands-on, interactive training session. Or book a sleepover with belugas.

A beluga whale

Our World Gallery

9 Prepare to be amazed and inspired by this introduction into the fascinating world of the Vancouver Aquarium and its exhibits. This gallery features an in-depth look at the ongoing research and conservation initiatives, which take place both onsite and in the field.

4-D Experience

10 Filled with thrilling sensory effects, this attraction combines the drama of a 3-D wildlife film with special effects, such as wind, water, scents, and more. Film schedules change daily.

For more information about the aquarium's sleepover programs, call 604 659 3504 or visit www.vanaqua.org/home

ⓣ⓪ Canada Place

Built for Expo '86 as the flagship Canada Pavilion, Canada Place is a Vancouver landmark. The roof's sail-like lines echo Canada's nautical roots. The "prow" extends well into the harbor. Following the highly successful world exhibition, which attracted more than 22 million visitors, Canada Place was transformed into a complex containing a cruise ship terminal, convention center, exhibition areas, and a first-class hotel. The promenade offers a terrific view of the city's harbor.

Patio, Café Pacifica

🍴 For casual dining, try the Café Pacifica in the Pan Pacific Hotel. Or, for a fine-dining experience, head to the hotel's Five Sails dinner-only restaurant. A food court across Canada Place Way is open until 9pm.

🅿 Underground pay parking is available at Canada Place. Less expensive parking can be found in the lot at the north foot of Burrard Street.

- 999 Canada Place Way
- Map L2
- 604 665 9000
- www.canadaplace.ca
- Open daily

Top 10 Features

1. Tourism Vancouver Visitor Centre
2. Architecture
3. Cruise Ship Terminal
4. Floatplanes
5. Community Events
6. FlyOver™ Canada
7. The Canadian Trail
8. Port Metro Vancouver's Discovery Centre
9. Vancouver Convention Centre
10. Heritage Horns

1 Tourism Vancouver Visitor Centre
Operated by Tourism Vancouver, this useful bureau located across Canada Place Way at 200 Burrard Street, on the plaza level, offers free brochures and city maps. The knowledgeable, multilingual volunteer staff will help you plan your stay in Vancouver.

2 Architecture
Built for Expo '86 on a former cargo dock, Canada Place's award-winning design is notable for the five Teflon-coated fiberglass sails, resembling a sailing ship in full rigging, suspended over the convention center.

3 Cruise Ship Terminal
The cruise ship terminal at Canada Place welcomes hundreds of thousands of visitors a year. The three-berth terminal is adjacent to the promenade, providing visitors with a close-up view. From the terminal, it's a short walk to the sights and shops of Gastown *(see pp60–5).*

Some of the largest and most luxurious ships afloat sail from Vancouver to Alaska; visit www.portmetrovancouver.com

Floatplanes
Pontooned planes arriving from Victoria land at Coal Harbour, to the west of Canada Place. Helicopters from Victoria descend on the east side of the complex.

Community Events
Canada Place hosts a variety of events celebrating the Canadian Spirit, ranging from free waterfront yoga classes and busker performances on summer weekends to Canada Day celebrations with fireworks every year on July 1 *(below)*.

FlyOver™ Canada
Visitors of all ages can soar from coast to coast on a breathtaking virtual journey that takes in the excitement and grandeur of Canada's landscape in the latest flight ride technology. Wind, sounds, and scents add to the experience.

The Canadian Trail
The trail *(below)* is a walk through Canadian history. Interactive exhibits highlight Canada's heritage, people, innovations, sports, and geography from the harbor days, impressive landscape and urban city.

Port Metro Vancouver's Discovery Centre
Learn about the port through interactive touch screen kiosks, displays, videos, and presentations located at the north end of Canada Place.

Expo '86

On May 2, 1986, Prince Charles and Princess Diana opened Expo '86, a hugely successful world's fair that hosted 50 per cent more people than expected. Unfortunately, it closed with a $311-million deficit. However, enduring legacies such as Canada Place (the former Canada Pavilion) Science World, the SkyTrain, and the urban renewal of a once-derelict area around False Creek, show that Expo '86 ultimately gave back to Vancouver much more than it had cost.

Vancouver Convention Centre
Conventions and exhibitions are housed in grand halls accessed by an indoor promenade that echoes the exterior walkway. The state-of-the-art, eco-designed facility hosts both conventions and consumer trade-shows, including the huge Vancouver Snow Show in October.

Heritage Horns
Every day, at noon, the sound of ten cast-aluminum air horns blasts across Vancouver and beyond from the top of Canada Place. Designed and built by Robert Swanson in 1967 as a project to celebrate Canada's 100th birthday, the first four notes of the noon hour blast are from the country's national anthem, *O Canada*.

Every July 1, Canada Day fireworks awe spectators with technically brilliant displays over the harbor at Canada Place

Top 10 Capilano Suspension Bridge Park

For thrill appeal, few sites rival Capilano Suspension Bridge Park. At the height that eagles fly, the bridge is a swaying span across the tumbling Capilano River far below. The world's longest and highest suspension footbridge, it crosses into the hushed recesses of a West Coast rainforest. This popular attraction now includes a walk high above the forest floor, from treetop to treetop, built using new technology. Scotsman George Grant MacKay, who bought the property in 1888, would be amazed. Today's modern bridge is the sixth on the site.

Costumed guides

🍴 Tasty salmon, beef, and chicken burgers are served at the Loggers' Grill. For coffees, pastries, and home-made pizzas, try the Canyon Café. For full-service, enjoy gourmet dining at the Bridge House Restaurant across Capilano Road.

✪ If heights are a concern when crossing the bridge, focus on the back of the person in front of you. It's well worth making the trip across.

• 3735 Capilano Rd, North Vancouver
• Map B1
• 604 985 7474
• www.capbridge.com
• Open 9am–5pm; Summer: 8:30am–dusk; closed Dec 25
• Adm: adults $34.95, seniors $32.95, students $28.95, youth (13–16) $21.95, children $12 (under 6s free)

Top 10 Features

1. Suspension Bridge
2. Locals from the Past
3. The Kia'palano Big House
4. Cliffwalk
5. Treetops Adventure
6. Treetops Technology
7. Totem Poles
8. Living Forest
9. Story Centre
10. English Country Garden

1 Suspension Bridge

This awe-inspiring bridge is built of sturdy steel cables spanning 450 ft (137 m) and strong enough to support a full Boeing 747. Those crossing the bridge today cling tightly to the handrails as they experience the same thrills as visitors did in 1889 *(center)*.

2 Locals from the Past

Friendly costumed guides in period attire welcome visitors to the park. Taking on the roles of local historical characters, the guides narrate the sometimes hair-raising stories of the North Shore's early days when timber was king.

3 The Kia'palano Big House

An interactive exhibit with storytelling and a First Nations interpreter is located in the open-fronted Little Big House

(a smaller version of the Big House). Skills and cultural knowledge are shared with appreciative onlookers. At the center of the cedar-planked Kia'palano Big House is the Next Generation story pole, honoring First Nations artists.

4 Cliffwalk
Almost 700 ft (213 m) of bridges and stairs lead along the cliff edge, offering stunning views of the Capilano River gorge 230 ft (70 m) below. Once on the other side, visitors can enjoy the panoramic views from the cantilevered deck that serves as a lookout.

5 Treetops Adventure
This exhilarating exhibit is located in the West Coast rainforest across the suspension bridge. A boardwalk leads you gently upwards over seven suspension bridges attached to eight old-growth Douglas fir trees (above). At the end of your journey, you are 100 ft (30 m) high in the mysterious zone of mid-story treetops.

6 Treetops Technology
To protect the delicate environment, Treetops Adventure uses an innovative compression system to secure observation platforms to the trees. Instead of nails or screws, friction collars are used. Held on by compression, they exert a gentle pressure equivalent to pressing a thumb firmly on a tabletop.

7 Totem Poles
At the centre's entrance, a gathering of totem poles carved by local Coast Salish First Nations people makes a colorful display (below). Introduced in the 1930s, the carved poles now number more than 30.

8 Living Forest
In the Living Forest ecology area, clever interactive displays educate about native plants and trees, such as Douglas firs. Panels feature the animals and bugs living in a West Coast rainforest. Naturalists offer guided tours year round on its peaceful forest trails.

9 Story Centre
From miners to loggers to dancehall girls, the centre tells the history of the park and of North Vancouver in a walk-through exhibit. Hundreds of photographs bring history to life, while captions put the people and places into perspective. Voices from the Past, an audio component, fills in any blanks.

10 English Country Garden
The picturesque perennial garden harks back to the homeland of many of Vancouver's early settlers. Planted in 1910, the azaleas and rhododendrons dazzle with massive colorful blooms. The shrubs are at their best in May.

A Lasting Legacy
Scotsman George Grant MacKay loved the outdoors. As Vancouver's first park commissioner, he voted in favor of Stanley Park in 1886. Two years later, he bought 9 sq miles (23 sq km) of old-growth forest along the Capilano River and built a cabin on the edge of the canyon wall. Then, with the help of local Coast Salish, he built a small hemp rope and cedar suspension bridge in 1889. This was the very first bridge.

🔟 University of British Columbia Museum of Anthropology

Founded in 1947 and located in a breathtaking setting, this museum houses one of the world's finest displays of Northwest Coast First Nations art. Here you'll also find European ceramics, Asian textiles, Greek and Roman pottery, and African masks, as well as full-size totem poles and contemporary carvings. All are housed in a 19th-century building designed by Arthur Erickson. The museum was greatly enhanced in 2010 with new laboratories, a research center, library and archive. Unique visible storage galleries bring some 10,000 objects to public view and changing exhibits highlight works by indigenous artists.

The impressive building that houses the museum

🛍 The museum shop is renowned for its outstanding selection of original gold and silver jewelry, prints, argillite, textiles, and other treasures.

🅿 Parking is available at the Rose Garden Parkade opposite the museum.

- 6393 NW Marine Drive
- Beyond Vancouver Map
- 604 822 5087
- www.moa.ubc.ca
- Open winter: 10am–5pm Tue–Sun (10am–9pm Tue); summer: 10am–5pm daily (10am–9pm Tue)
- Adm: adults $16.75, senior/students $14.50, under 6s free. Tue (5pm–9pm): $9 flat rate (includes groups)

Top 10 Highlights

1. Welcome Figure
2. Carved Doors
3. Bentwood Boxes
4. Weaving
5. Ceramic Stove
6. Totem Poles
7. The Raven and The First Men
8. Athenian Black Band Cup
9. New Guinea Necklaces
10. Haida Houses

Welcome Figure
1 On the museum's outdoor welcome plaza stands a red cedar welcome figure holding a *fisher* (an animal believed to have healing powers). This and other contemporary work, including a stylized mosaic of colored granite, were created by Musqueam artist Susan Point.

Carved Doors
2 These massive doors *(below left)* were carved out of red cedar in 1976 by master Gitxsan First Nations artists from the 'Ksan cultural center. They depict the history of the first people of the Skeena River region in British Columbia.

Bentwood Boxes
3 These boxes, which can be used for cooking as well as storage, are made in a very special way. The four sides are composed of one piece of cedar, which is notched in three places, steamed, and bent to form the shape of the box before the base is attached.

Weaving

One of the blankets on display was woven using sheep's wool by Robyn and Debra Sparrow of the Musqueam First Nation (1997). Weaving is an important art form for Salish peoples, re-vitalized as a practice in the 1960s by several First Nations women.

Ceramic Stove

The centerpiece of the Koerner Ceramics Gallery is a stove *(left)* from Central or Eastern Europe, circa 1500–1600. Its lead-glazed tiles (from which heat would emanate after being stoked) depict popular religious figures of the time.

Totem Poles

Showcased beneath the 49-ft (15-m) glass walls of the Great Hall are towering totem poles *(center)* from many First Nations. The glass and concrete structure of the hall provides a perfect setting for the poles.

Key to Floor plan

▦	Koerner European Ceramic Gallery
▦	Great Hall
▦	Bill Reid Rotunda
▦	Multiversity Galleries

New Guinea Necklaces

These ornate necklaces form part of the museum's founding collection of South Pacific materials, donated to the museum in 1927 by Canadian explorer Frank Burnett.

Haida Houses

Two full-size Haida Houses stand outside this fascinating museum, overlooking the water, surrounded by a forest of soaring, full-scale totem poles. They were designed in 1962 by contemporary Haida artist Bill Reid and Namgis artist Doug Cramer and make for a breathtaking sight.

The Raven and the First Men

This massive sculpture *(below)*, carved from a block of 106 laminated yellow cedar planks by Haida artist Bill Reid, is one of the most famous carvings in the world. It depicts the figure of Raven (a wise and powerful yet mischievous trickster) discovering the first Haida humans and coaxing them out into the world from a giant clamshell.

Athenian Black Band Cup

Housed in the classical Greek and Roman pottery collection, this cup was made in Greece, circa 540–530 B.C. It is attributed to the "Centaur Painter," one of a group of artists known for decorating scores of drinking cups used by men of Athens at famous (and also sometimes notorious) symposia or loud drinking parties.

Going Underground

The museum is built on three gun emplacements, which were incorporated into the design of the building. Used during World War II, two bunkers are located outside the grounds, one of which is the platform for Bill Reid's "Raven" carving. Beneath the building a maze of secret tunnels connects the bunkers. These are strictly closed to the public.

🔟 Vancouver Art Gallery

The Vancouver Art Gallery is the largest art gallery in Western Canada, and with the most significant collection of works by Emily Carr, BC's preeminent artist and writer, it is well worth the entry fee. The gallery specializes in impressive national and international exhibitions, with innovative approaches to old masters as well as contemporary visionaries. The gallery's collection comprises more than 10,000 works, including a large collection of photo-based art by Vancouver's international art superstar Jeff Wall and renowned Haida artist Robert Davidson. Housed in a NeoClassical heritage building redesigned by acclaimed local architect Arthur Erickson, the gallery opened in 1983.

Rotunda

🔘 The Gallery Café patio is a gem on sunny summer days. You do not need to purchase admission to the gallery to eat at the café.

🔘 The Gallery Store sells contemporary art books, posters, paper goods, jewelry, and giftware, including a wide selection of Emily Carr merchandise.

- *750 Hornby St*
- *Map K3*
- *604 662 4700*
- *www.vanartgallery. bc.ca*
- *Open 10am–9pm Tue; 10am–5:30pm Wed–Mon*
- *Adm: adult $19.50, seniors (65+) $14, students $13, children $7 (under 5s free). By donation 5pm–9pm Tue, members free*

Top 10 Features

1. Court House Building
2. Emily Carr Collection
3. Art on the Rooftop
4. Photoconceptual Collection
5. Southern Façade
6. Exhibitions Program
7. Jeff Wall Collection
8. Architecture
9. First Nations Art
10. Family Programming

Court House Building

Built in 1912 as the Provincial Court House, the building reflects the imposing style of the era's leading Canadian architect, Francis Rattenbury.

Emily Carr Collection

The Gallery holds more than 200 works by Emily Carr. This renowned West Coast artist studied local Native cultures, capturing their way of life in her paintings. Haida artifacts such as totem poles were a common subject. Stormy West Coast colors as seen, for example, in *Logger's Culls (center)*, dominate her work. Items such as her tiny sketch book are also on display.

Art on the Rooftop

Vancouver artist Ken Lum's innovative *Four Boats Stranded: Red and Yellow, Black and White* stands out on the gallery's roof *(above)*. The installations include a scaled-down version of a First Nations longboat.

➡️ *Tours of the gallery are free with admission and take place on Thursdays and Sundays throughout the year*

Photoconceptual Collection

The gallery is known for its permanent collection of contemporary photo-based art that spans two decades and includes works by the Vancouver School of artists, such as Jeff Wall, Stan Douglas, Ian Wallace, and Ken Lum, as well as international artists Nancy Spero and Cindy Sherman, among others.

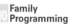

PLACED UPON THE HORIZON (CASTING SHADOWS)

Southern Façade

Overlooking Robson Street, the original steps into the court house are now a popular meeting spot for locals. On the portico *(above)* is a cryptic message carved in yellow cedar letters by conceptual artist Lawrence Weiner.

Exhibitions Program

Foremost artists, ranging from historic masters to leading-edge contemporary artists, are regularly presented in major thematic exhibitions, solo shows, and intimate, focused showcases.

Jeff Wall Collection

Some of celebrated photographic artist Jeff Wall's large backlit photographs in the gallery's collection measure up to 12 feet (4 meters) wide.

Architecture

Architectural icon Arthur Erickson added 41,400 sq ft (3,715 sq m) of exhibit space to the old court house when transforming it into the gallery's permanent home. Erickson retained many of the original features, including the courtroom, with its carved judge's bench.

First Nations Art

Paintings, carvings, and sculpture by Pacific Northwest Native artists are part of the gallery's rotating permanent collection, which includes sculptures by late Haida master carver Bill Reid *(see p36)*. Reflecting the modernist style of many Native artists, *Eagles (below)*, by Haida artist Robert Davidson, combines principles of abstraction with traditional iconography.

Family Programming

The gallery makes art accessible to younger visitors with family-focused activites every Saturday and every other Sunday, as well as three "mega" family-oriented weekends each year.

Emily Carr

Emily Carr was born into a wealthy Victoria family in 1871. The eccentric artist, however, chose a bohemian lifestyle, and her powerful artworks were painted on a pauper's budget, often in the old-growth forests of Haida Gwaii (Queen Charlotte Islands). It wasn't until 1937, when Carr was 65 years old, that the Vancouver Art Gallery bought one of her works. Largely overlooked during her lifetime, Carr's works now command some of the highest prices in Canada.

Exhibitions are enhanced with lectures by gallery curators, artists, and art historians; call 604 662 4717 for details

TOP 10 Granville Island

Bustling Granville Island attracts millions of visitors every year, and rightly so. Where heavy industries once belched noxious fumes, street entertainers now amuse passersby with music, comedy, and magic. The Granville Island Public Market offers an enchanting mix of edibles and collectibles. More than 200 shops scattered throughout the Island sell everything from custom-made jewelry to yachts.

Aquabus

🍴 La Baguette et l'Echalote, adjacent to the market, at 1680 Johnston St, is one of the best French patisseries in town.

☀ Locals know that the doors, and most businesses, inside the public market building are unofficially open by 8am. Arrive early if you want a sneak peek before the market gets busy.

The summer-only Water Park is free. Find it just off Cartwright Street (see p46).

- Map H5
- 604 666 6655
- www.granville island.com
- Public market: open 9am–7pm daily; closed Dec 25 & 26, Jan 1, Mon in Jan
- Net Loft and Kids Market: open 10am–7pm daily; varying hrs for businesses
- Edible Canada tours: www.ediblecanada.com

Top 10 Features

1. Granville Island Public Market
2. Marina and Maritime Market
3. Kids Market
4. New-Small and Sterling Studio Glass
5. Railspur District
6. Granville Island Brewing Co.
7. Edible Canada
8. Net Loft
9. Arts Club Theatre and Lounge
10. Crafthouse

Marina and Maritime Market
Shops and services at the market include a kayak center *(above)*, seafood merchants, tours, boat rentals, and marine souvenir shops. At the marina, yachts and sailboats are moored beside rustic fishing boats.

Kids Market
Clowns and magicians guarantee fun in a fantasyland for children. More than 20 shops sell everything from games and toys to pint-sized clothing.

Granville Island Public Market
The centerpiece of the island's shopping experience, the public market is an irresistible emporium of green grocers, butchers, bakers, fishmongers, importers, stalls selling ethnic foods, craft vendors, sweet stands, florists, and casual eateries *(center)*. It also has a micro-roaster of organic coffee.

New-Small and Sterling Studio Glass
Watch David New-Small and apprentices as they blow molten glass into beautiful vases, ornaments, jewelry, and dishes using traditional techniques. One of four furnaces keeps 150 lbs (70 kg) of glass molten at 2,000˚F (1,100˚C) around the clock. Visit the adjoining gallery to admire or buy handmade glass jewelry, ornaments, bowls, vases, and plates.

Free parking on the Island is from one to three hours; pay parking at the east end avoids the very real possibility of a parking ticket

Railspur District
5️⃣ The cozy artisan studio-shops *(above)* in this small laneway are operated by painters, potters, and craftspeople specializing in wood, fabric, leather, glass, and industrial cast-offs.

Granville Island Brewing Company
6️⃣ This microbrewery – Canada's first – opened in 1984. Sample the delicious beers made using only natural ingredients at many Vancouver pubs or in the brewery's Taproom after a behind-the-scenes tour, offered daily at noon, 2pm, and 4pm.

Edible Canada
7️⃣ Here you'll find the best of what Canadian producers have to offer, from specialist cheeses and homemade soups to locally-distilled sake and many other artisan food products, all of which make unique gifts to take home *(right)*. Stop off at the bistro to enjoy an ever-changing menu of seasonal delights or book one of the fascinating foodie tours of Chinatown or the public market.

Crafthouse
🔟 Crafthouse gallery and shop showcases contemporary fine crafts shaped by innovation and excellence, including sculptures, furniture, jewelry, kitchenware, and bowls *(right)*. The pieces are created by both emerging and established artists who are Canadian members of the Craft Council of British Columbia (CCBC).

Net Loft
8️⃣ An intimate collection of boutiques sells unusual souvenirs, such as handmade paper, hats, offbeat postcards, beads of all kinds, and local and First Nations crafts.

Arts Club Theatre and Lounge
9️⃣ The Arts Club Theatre Company produces contemporary comedies and new works to classics at the Granville Island Stage. The casual Backstage Lounge showcases local bands *(see p43 and p82)*.

Granville Island Ferries

The small vessels of the Aquabus and False Creek Ferries fleets provide year-round service around False Creek, with frequent sailings to and from downtown. They are a fun way to travel to Granville Island. Other routes include stops at Science World, Yaletown, and Vanier Park. Mini sunset cruises are also available.

False Creek Ferries (604 684 7781) and Aquabus (604 689 5858) vessels depart the west and north sides of the market respectively

21

🔟 Science World

Fascinating insights into all aspects of the universe are featured at the award-winning Science World at TELUS World of Science. Explorations begin with the smallest insect and progress to the farthest corners of the galaxy. A legacy of Expo '86, the building opened as a science center in 1989 after passionate community efforts. Seven galleries feature hundreds of delightfully interactive, hands-on displays and exhibits, while intriguing traveling exhibits show regularly. A $35 million renovation has added more than 14,000 sq ft (1,300 sq m) of gallery space for even more creative exploration.

Search Gallery

🍴 White Spot, a popular BC chain known for its burgers slathered with Triple O (triple oozy) sauce, is on the Science World site. A concession on Level 2 offers juices, popcorn, and ice cream bars.

🅿 Paid parking in the small lot is at a premium. It's best to take the SkyTrain to Main Street Station, then walk the short block to Science World.

- 1455 Quebec St
- Map M5
- 604 443 7440
- www.scienceworld.ca
- Open summer: 10am–6pm daily; winter: 10am–5pm Mon–Fri, 10am–6pm Sat–Sun, holidays; closed Dec 25
- Adm: adults $21, seniors/students/youth (13–18) $17.25, children $14.25 (under 4s free). Additional fee for OMNIMAX® Theatre

Top 10 Highlights

1. Geodesic Dome
2. OMNIMAX® Theatre
3. Search Gallery
4. Kidspace Gallery
5. Peter Brown Family Centre Stage
6. Our World Gallery
7. Feature Gallery
8. Eureka! Gallery
9. Science Theatre
10. BodyWorks Gallery

1 Geodesic Dome

Science World's 155-ft- (47-m-) tall geodesic dome *(center)* is affectionately dubbed "the golf ball" by locals. The design is based on the prototype structure made famous by US inventor and architect R. Buckminster Fuller. Mirrorlike exterior panels, 766 in all, reflect the sunlight, while 391 exterior lights sparkle at night.

2 OMNIMAX® Theatre

The five-story screen – one of the largest in the world – envelops viewers with thrilling films such as Academy Award-nominated *The Living Sea*. The 400-seat theater, located in the geodesic dome, projects images nine times larger than a conventional movie house onto a screen 88 ft (27 m) in diameter. Sound pours out of 28 digital speakers.

3 Search: The Sara Stern Gallery

Explore natural history with live critters and creepy crawlies, a beaver-home replica, a real bee colony, and a life-size Tyrannosaurus rex skeleton cast.

4 Kidspace Gallery

Kids ages two to six get to burn off excess energy climbing, sliding, running, and jumping on the exhibits *(below)*. Water play, with boats supplied, is a favorite.

A four-hour visit is the average at Science World

Entrance

Peter Brown Family Centre Stage
Scientific principles and phenomena are explored in five daily shows. Presenters mix balloons and electricity, bubbles and fire to dazzle and captivate as well as teach. Volunteer kids are invited on stage.

Key to Floor plan
	Level 1
	Level 2
	Level 3

Science Theatre
Everything from cartoons for toddlers to shows and movies for the whole family – about science, nature, and outer space. High definition reveals the smallest details in the featured short films shown here.

BodyWorks Gallery
BodyWorks encourages a positive curiosity about the human body. Questions about how human beings hear and smell are answered in this fun-filled interactive space. Strength and dexterity are tested by activities such as bike pedaling and simulated skiing.

Our World Gallery
As you check out what has been left in the garbage dump or walk into a giant cheese burger, Our World reveals how the choices we make about waste disposal, food production, and transportation affect our home communities.

Feature Gallery
The best in traveling exhibitions are showcased here. Always fresh and exciting, the content of the gallery changes every few months but consistently offers hands-on interactive opportunities for all ages to explore science topics that encompass light, sound, engineering, and more.

Eureka! Gallery
Eureka! Gallery *(above)* explores universal themes such as water, air, motion, and invention. Children and adults alike are invited to make their own discoveries in a lifelike science laboratory environment. Use the infrared camera to discover the hot spots on your body.

Museum Guide
Science World's first floor is home to Puzzles and Our World. On the second floor are the Eureka!, Contraption Corner, Kidspace, Search: The Sara Stern Gallery, and the Feature Gallery. OMNIMAX® Theatre, on the third floor, is accessible with a Science World ticket or independently by way of a separate entrance to the building.

TOP 10 Royal British Columbia Museum

Founded in Victoria in 1886, this impressive museum focuses on BC's cultures, history, geography, flora, and fauna. The museum is regarded as one of the best in Canada for the striking way it presents its exhibits. It has about 26,000 sq ft (2,415 sq m) of exhibition space and houses more than seven million items in its collection. Dramatic walk-through scenarios bring history to life in four galleries, each featuring original and often rarely seen artifacts. The museum's collection of First Nations art and traditional objects is one of the largest and most impressive in the world.

Helmcken House

🔵 Opposite the coat-check, the Museum Café specializes in fine coffees, lattes, and pastries. Or try a light-lunch salad or sandwich.

🔵 Pay parking is located behind the museum on Superior Street.

Pick up a free map of the museum at the entrance.

- 675 Belleville St, Victoria
- Map P4
- 1 888 447 7977
- www.royalbc museum.bc.ca
- Open 10am–5pm daily; closed Jan 1 & Dec 25
- Adm: adults $16, seniors/youth/students $10, family $42 (under 5s free)
- Helmcken House & St. Ann's Schoolhouse open noon–4pm May–Labor Day (early Sep); included in museum adm

Top 10 Features

1. St. Ann's Schoolhouse
2. Ocean Station
3. Natural History Gallery
4. First Peoples Gallery
5. History Gallery
6. Helmcken House
7. Netherlands Centennial Carillon Tower
8. Mungo Martin House
9. IMAX Victoria Theatre
10. Thunderbird Park

1 St. Ann's Schoolhouse

Built in 1844 and donated to the museum by the Sisters of St. Ann, this building was once a school classroom. It was moved to its current location in 1974 and is now an interpretive center.

2 Ocean Station

A Victorian-era "submarine" exhibit allows visitors to access BC's coastal marine life. Peer through portholes at kelp beds, watch live sea creatures, including sea urchins and fish, in the central 95-gallon (360-liter) aquarium, then check out the colorful vistas on a giant underwater cliff *(above)* through a moveable periscope.

3 Natural History Gallery

Realistic dioramas explore a range of environments, from ocean to boreal forest, including the giant old-growth forest that once covered coastal BC. One of the best of a range of animals depicted in re-created habitats is a grizzly bear, BC's largest land predator.

Mammoth roamed the cold lands 25,000 to 12,000 years ago

First Peoples Gallery
Historic photos, video, audio, and Native artifacts are combined for a spellbinding experience *(above)*. Look out for the collection of superb ceremonial masks.

Key to Plan

	Ground floor
	Second floor
	Third floor

History Gallery
In the atmospheric 20th-Century Hall, it's easy to step back into the Victoria of the early 1900s *(right)*. Re-created buildings include the Grand Hotel, with its authentic wood-cobbled street, a salmon cannery, a dressmaker's studio, and a Chinese herbalist's shop, all displaying authentic period objects. Soft lighting sets the mood.

Mungo Martin House
Also called Wawadit'la, this replica of a big house was built in 1952 by Chief Mungo Martin, who was considered the finest carver of his day, with the assistance of his family. The house posts bear the family's crest. Wawadit'la is a functioning big house which is still used for First Nations events with the permission of Chief Martin's grandson.

Thunderbird Park
A dozen poles preside over this park. The carved mythical figures tell stories of traditional Coast Salish cultures. Included are Gitxsan memorial poles, Haida mortuary poles, a Cumshewa pole, and Kwakwaka'wakw heraldic poles.

Helmcken House
One of the oldest houses in BC still on its original site was built by Dr. John Sebastian Helmcken in 1852. The three-room log structure is made of Douglas fir trees. Period furnishings reflect the Victorian era.

Netherlands Centennial Carillon Tower
The tower, which has 62 bells, was gifted to the museum in 1967 from BC residents of Dutch descent. Free recitals are held at 3pm on Sundays.

IMAX Victoria Theatre
Subjects as diverse as whales and outer space are explored in the rotating series of documentary and feature films on the theater's six-story screen.

Museum Guide

The main exhibits are located on the second and third floors of the museum. Natural History Gallery and the temporary exhibition gallery are on the second floor, the First Nations and History galleries on the third. More sites are found outside.

Near the carillon tower, the entrance to the museum-operated BC Archives has been beautified with plants native to the province

Around Long Beach

The wild west coast of Vancouver Island's Long Beach area offers pristine wilderness, old-growth rainforest, endless beaches, and mystical vistas. Bald eagles appear in large numbers in Clayoquot Sound, a UNESCO biosphere reserve, while the Pacific Ocean teems with Dall's porpoises, sea lions, and seals. Surfing, fishing, kayaking, and storm watching are superb.

Boogie boarders, Long Beach

🍴 Try local oysters, Dungeness crab, halibut, and wild salmon when in the Long Beach area. Schooner Restaurant in Tofino (331 Campbell St, 250 725 3444) showcases Vancouver Island's seafood and perfectly aged meat. Ucluelet's Norwoods Restaurant (1714 Peninsula Rd, 250 726 7001) serves contemporary West Coast cuisine.

📅 Book early for the weeklong Pacific Rim Whale Festival (250 726 7798, www.pacific rimwhalefestival.com) in late March.

• Map A4
• Tourist information: www.tourismtofino.com and www.ucluelet.travel

Top 10 Sights

1. Kwisitis Visitor Centre
2. Tofino
3. Long Beach
4. Clayoquot Sound
5. Meares Island
6. Eagle Aerie Gallery
7. Pacific Rim National Park Reserve of Canada
8. Ucluelet
9. Wild Pacific Trail
10. West Coast Trail

Tofino

Tofino was named by Spanish explorer Juan Francisco de la Bodega y Quadra after one of his teachers, a hydrographer. Located at the entrance to Clayoquot Sound, this pretty coastal town, with 1,600 residents, provides easy access to white-sand beaches and is a magnet for outdoor adventurers, winter storm watchers, and foodies. At the government docks *(center)*, seafood is sold right off the boats.

Kwisitis Visitor Centre

The cedar-built center makes a great first stop for Long Beach visitors. Indoor displays introduce natural history as well as historic cultural objects of the local Nuu-Chah-Nulth people. Step out on the viewing platform to spot whales passing along the coast. Not to be missed are the center's beach tours.

Long Beach

Rolling waves wash the white sand shores of this seemingly endless wind-swept beach, 15.5 mi (25 km) in length *(below)*. The crashing Pacific Ocean rollers offer unbeatable year-round surfing. Giant Sitka spruce and cedars growing in moss-draped temperate rainforests border the beach.

→ *Allow about six hours for the slow but scenic 200-mile (320-km) drive from Victoria to Tofino along Highways 1 and 4*

Clayoquot Sound
Pronounced "cla-kwat", Clayoquot boasts trees 295 ft (90 m) tall and 1,700 years old. The UNESCO biosphere reserve shares the territory with black bears, elk *(above)*, wolves, and an elusive endangered bird, the marbled murrelet. The coastline mingles bays, beaches, channels, intertidal lagoons, and mudflats.

Meares Island
Accessed by boat or water taxi, Meares Island is popular for boat and kayak tours, followed by a stroll along Boardwalk Trail to the hanging garden tree. Birdlife abounds along the island's shores.

Eagle Aerie Gallery
The tranquil cedar-planked Eagle Aerie Gallery in Tofino is a hand-hewn longhouse with a carved and painted housefront traditional to the local First Nations people. Internationally acclaimed Tsimshian printmaker Roy Henry Vickers is the gallerist, and his artwork is also on sale here *(below)*.

Pacific Rim National Park Reserve of Canada
A world-famous area for whale-watching, the 80-mi- (130-km) long park is made up of three distinct areas: Long Beach, the West Coast Trail, and the Broken Group Islands *(see p101)*.

Ucluelet
This small town is the gateway to multiple outdoor activities on both land and water. Avid fishers flock here for steelhead, sturgeon, halibut, and Pacific and freshwater salmon. The climate is temperate, with 328 frost-free days a year.

Wild Pacific Trail
This breathtaking 10-mi (16-km) trail runs alongside the Pacific Ocean through coastal rainforest, from the tip of the Ucluelet peninsula to the Pacific Rim National Park. Hikers are surrounded by lush stands of conifers in the largest lowland temperate rainforest on earth.

West Coast Trail
The West Coast Trail is a challenging 46-mi (75-km) hike along a historic trail built to aid the rescue of shipwrecked mariners. The trail hugs the shoreline where approximately 65 ships met their demise. Rocky headlands along the trail are dotted with caves, arches, and waterfalls.

Gray Whales
Each year, an estimated 22,000 gray whales migrate past the Vancouver Island coast around Long Beach. They're on an 11,000-mi (17,700-km) round trip, migrating south from the Arctic to their breeding grounds off southern California and Mexico from December to early February, and returning north from March through May.

Reservations and permits are required for the West Coast Trail, which can be hiked in part or full (seven days); call 250 726 4453

🔟 Whistler

The 75-mile (120-km) drive to Whistler from Vancouver reveals stunning scenery, a combination of Howe Sound's sparkling blue waters and the majestic snow-covered Coast Mountain range. Welcoming more than two million visitors each year, the side-by-side peaks of Whistler and Blackcomb mountains are magnificent. A year-round resort, Whistler has hosted the Olympic and Paralympic Winter Games. While the resort is known for its exemplary accommodations and over 90 restaurants and 200 shops, it still preserves natural enclaves of forests and five lakes.

Chalet, Upper Village

🍽 Horstman Hut is the uppermost eatery in the area, sitting at 7,494 ft (2,284 m) on Blackcomb Mountain.

🚡 Ride PEAK 2 PEAK from Whistler to Blackcomb Mountains on the highest and longest gondola of its type in the world.

For free information, visit the Whistler Visitor Information Centre. 201-4230 Gateway Dr; 604 935 3357.

Take warm clothing up the mountains, even in summer.

• Map F1
• www.whistler.com
• Whistler Activity and Information Centre, 4010 Whistler Way, 604 935 3357 or 1 877 991 9988
• Whistler Central Reservations: 604 664 5625 or 1 800 944 7853

Top 10 Features

1. Whistler Mountain
2. Blackcomb Mountain
3. Whistler Village
4. Alta Lake
5. Upper Village
6. Valley Trail
7. Fairmont Chateau Whistler
8. Green Lake
9. Creekside
10. Village North

1 Whistler Mountain

Skiers and snowboarders enjoy 7.4 sq miles (19.3 sq km) of impressive terrain with over 100 marked trails *(center)*. Whistler Village Gondola offers superb views of Whistler Valley during the 20-minute ride to the top. Mountain biking and alpine hiking are exceptional summer activities. Mountain-top restaurants offer everything from snacks to fine dining.

2 Blackcomb Mountain

Blackcomb, nicknamed the "Mile High Mountain," towers over Whistler resort at an elevation of 7,494 ft (2,284 m). Skiers and snowboarders ride to more than 100 marked runs from three bases. In summer, a sightseeing trip to Horstman Glacier is not to be missed. Or take advantage of the glacier's superb summer skiing and snowboarding.

3 Whistler Village

This pedestrian-only Alpine-style enclave ringed by shops, hotels, and restaurants *(below)* provides ski-in, ski-out access to Whistler Mountain. It's busy round the clock with skiers and boarders heading to the mountain, diners on patios, and late-night clubgoers.

There are several breathtaking stops along the scenic "sea to sky" drive to Whistler – take your time

4 Alta Lake
Alta Lake was once home to Rainbow Lodge, Whistler's first resort. Traces of the lodge remain at Rainbow Park *(above)*, a delightful picnic spot. Explore the lake's perimeter along the paved Valley Trail, or swim, wind surf, or canoe.

8 Green Lake
A glacial gem with crystal clear water courtesy of mountain melt, Green Lake is truly green. It is a firm favorite of canoeists, with views taking in some of the area's highest peaks, including massive Mount Currie.

9 Creekside
A multi-million dollar investment has transformed this activity center, providing glamorous hotels and a mini-mall. Skiers can access Whistler Mountain from this historic base at the Creekside Gondola.

5 Upper Village
Nestled at the base of Blackcomb Mountain, the Upper Village offers easy access to the slopes. It leads past skaters. It leads past Lost Lake, Rainbow Park, luxury hotels, award-winning restaurants, and quality shops here are unsurpassed. In summer, Adventure Zone provides endless options for kids.

10 Village North
Construction of Village North followed that of Upper Village, with the added attractions of vehicle access, a shopping mall complete with The Marketplace – one of the resort's best grocery stores – cafés, restaurants, and intriguing shops.

6 Valley Trail
This 12-mile (20-km) Valley Trail attracts walkers, cyclists, and in-line skaters. It leads past Lost Lake, Rainbow Park, and Alta, Nita, and Alpha lakes, through stands of trees fringing residential areas. In winter, the Lost Lake loop is dedicated to cross-country skiing.

7 Fairmont Chateau Whistler
Whistler's grand dame *(above)* reigns over the valley from the Upper Village. The antique furnishings, gold-leaf ceiling painting, and Canadian art in the lobby of this chateau-style hotel make it well worth a visit. The opulent Mallard Bar has a popular heated patio.

Whistler Transit
A free shuttle service runs every 20 to 30 minutes between village hotels and condos to the ski slopes. WAVE, the municipal bus service, transports visitors to and from the villages and around the town. For a taxi, call 604 932 3333.

For a glimpse into Whistler's pioneer history, visit Whistler Museum & Archives, 4333 Main St, Village North; call 604 932 2019

Left **Fairmont Chateau Whistler Golf Course** Right **Snowboarding, Blackcomb Mountain**

Fun Things to Do in Whistler

Skiing
Whistler and Blackcomb cater to all ages and levels of skiers. With over 30 ft (10 m) of snow fall yearly, boosted by snowmaking, the winter season provides over 100 runs. Summer skiing on Blackcomb's glacier.

Golf
Known as the "Big Four," Whistler's four golf courses take advantage of their mountain settings, with lakes, creeks, rolling greens, and mountain views. Golfers are pampered with deluxe facilities and fine dining. ◈ *Whistler Central Reservations: 1 800 944 7853*

Black bear cub

Dog Sledding
The distinctly northern activity of dog sledding, with energetic huskies eager to pull their sleds through the backcountry, is suitable for both adults and kids who enjoy mushing seven-dog teams. All proceeds are donated to the sled dog foundation.

Snowmobiling and Snowcat Tours
Speedy snowmobiles are an exhilarating way to see Blackcomb Mountain, or try the more sedate, heated Snowcat. A pleasant dinner at the alpine Crystal Hut can be added. ◈ *Canadian Snowmobile Adventures: 604 938 1616*

Snowboarding
Annual upgrades at the thrilling terrain parks ensure bigger and better rails and pipes for the advanced. Well-designed novice areas also.

Bear Watching
An intimate, respectful view of Whistler's black bears is offered on tours led by local bear researcher Michael Allen. Fifty or so bears live in the area's old-growth forests, feeding on the grassy mountain slopes and foraging for berries. Allen's tours provide an up-close look at bear habits and habitats suitable for all ages.

Mountain Biking
Free-flowing runs as well as technically demanding trails, groomed to perfection. Practice comes easy at the Mountain Bike Park, with its three Skills Centres, and jumps and learning tools for all levels.

Mountain biker, Whistler Mountain

Whistler and Blackcomb's winter ski season runs from late November to May

Whistler's Pioneers

Before Whistler Valley became a ski destination, the area was a magnet for explorers, miners, loggers, and pioneer entrepreneurs such as Alex and Myrtle Philip. The young American couple arrived in 1912, and two years later opened a fishing lodge on Alta Lake. Rainbow Lodge was soon BC's premiere resort destination, with visitors arriving on the now defunct Pacific Great Eastern Railway. The lodge burned down in 1977, but one of Rainbow Park's original guest log cabins and a replica of Alex's romantic Bridge of Sighs mark where it once stood.

Rainbow Lodge
The resort's main lodge was built from handcut and peeled logs. By its peak, 45 buildings had been constructed. Only four original cabins remain.

Alpine Sightseeing

Snowy peaks, glaciers, and glimpses of Whistler's namesake, the hoary marmot, or "whistler," make summer hikes memorable. Whistler's 30 miles (48 km) of marked trails are easy to follow. Refresh at the Roundhouse Lodge. The open-chair ascent to Horstman Glacier *(see p28)* is thrilling.

Adventure Zone

Parents and children play together in the exciting Blackcomb Base Adventure Zone in the Upper Village. Not to be missed is the child-sized Westcoaster Luge track snaking down the mountain. Other activities include the climbing center, bungee ride, and Spin Cycle, an astronaut-inspired ride.

Canoeing and Whitewater Rafting

Resort pioneer Alex Philip began the canoeing craze on picturesque Alta Lake. It's still a low-key way to spend a hot summer day. Canoe rentals and guided tours available. For a faster pace, whitewater raft the Green, Birkenhead, and Elaho rivers. ⊛ *Canoeing: Whistler Outdoor Experience: 604 932 3389 • Whistler River Adventures: 604 932 3532*

For details on activities at Whistler and Blackcomb, including bear watching, call 1 800 WHISTLER or visit www.whistler.com

Left **Chinese Cultural Centre Museum & Archives** Right **Museum of Vancouver**

Museums & Art Galleries

1 UBC Museum of Anthropology

Situated on cliffs overlooking Burrard Inlet, this airy museum houses over 500,000 ethnographic and archaeological objects from around the world, with emphasis on coastal First Nations *(see pp16–17).* ✆ *6393 NW Marine Dr • Map A2 • 604 822 5087 • Open 11am–9pm Tue, 11–5pm Wed–Sun • Adm*

The Raven and the First Men, UBC Museum of Anthropology

2 Vancouver Art Gallery

The Vancouver Art Gallery's growing collection is rich in historic and contemporary works by BC and international artists, including the world's largest grouping of Emily Carr pieces. The splendid *fin-de-siècle* exhibition hall hosts traveling exhibits *(see pp18–19).*

3 Vancouver Police Museum

An intriguing glimpse into the dark world of crime and punishment in Vancouver's past, including a walking tour. The 20,000 artifacts housed in the old Coroner's Court include confiscated weapons, counterfeit bills, and displays depicting scientific evidence. You may find yourself amid a gaggle of wide-eyed children, as school tours play an important part of programming. ✆ *240 E Cordova St • Map M4 • 604 665 3346 • Open 9am–5pm Mon–Sat (& Sun in summer) • Adm*

4 Chinese Cultural Centre Museum and Archives

Part of the Chinese Cultural Centre, the museum and archives share traditional Chinese architecture. The collection tells of the Chinese community from the Cariboo Gold Rush of the 1860s to the settlement of Chinatown. The annex exhibits classical and contemporary Chinese art. ✆ *555 Columbia St • Map M4 • 604 658 8880 • Open Tue–Sun 11am–5pm • Adm*

5 Museum of Vancouver

Permanent and short-term exhibits offer intimate looks at Vancouver's heritage. Hands-on exhibits, such as the 1950s soda shop, and a visit to the hippie era in Vancouver – complete with '60s clothes to try on – make recent history a delight *(see p79).*

The Crab, by G. Norris, Museum of Vancouver

Previous pages **The Wickaninnish Inn near Long Beach, Vancouver Island** *(see p116)*

6 Charles H. Scott Gallery

This public art gallery has a mandate to promote visual education and dialogue to a wide audience, including students, the arts community, and visitors alike. Shows feature innovative art of emerging and established artists, both local and international. ◈ 1399 Johnston St • Map H5 • 604 844 3809 • Open noon–5pm Mon–Fri, 10am–5pm Sat–Sun • Adm

7 BC Sports Hall of Fame and Museum

BC's sports achievements, including those of local heroes Terry Fox and his Marathon of Hope, and Rick Hansen's Man in Motion World Tour, are celebrated in 20,000 sq ft (1,858 sq m) of gallery space. The Participation Gallery entices visitors to try pitching, sprinting, and rock climbing. ◈ Gate A, BC Place • Map L4–L5 • 604 687 5520 • Open 10am–5pm daily • Adm

8 Vancouver Maritime Museum

Exhibits of artifacts, models, vessels, and photos pay tribute to Canada's marine heritage. At the heart of the collection is the restored 104-ft (32-m) schooner St. Roch, the second ship to navigate the North West Passage, but the first to travel it from west to east (see p77).

Wolf pendant, Bill Reid Gallery

9 Bill Reid Gallery

Bill Reid was one of Canada's greatest artists whose work helped introduce the art traditions of the Haida and the cultures of the Northwest Coast to a wider audience. The gallery houses more than 60 pieces of his jewelry (above), and works by contemporary Aboriginal artists. ◈ 639 Hornby St • Map K3 • 604 682 3455 • Open: 11am–5pm Wed–Sun

10 Inuit Gallery

One of the region's most respected commercial galleries, showing an outstanding, museum-quality selection of Inuit and North West Coast Native sculpture, graphics, and jewelry. ◈ 206 Cambie St • Map L3 • 604 688 7323 • Open 10am–6pm Mon-Sat, 11am–5pm Sun

Left **Carved doors, Museum of Anthropology** Right **Kwakwaka'wakw totem pole, Thunderbird Park**

TOP10 First Nations Art

1 'Ksan Mural
Five artists carved this red cedar frieze to illustrate Northwest Coast raven myths. The nine panels tell stories of how the Raven created the elements of the world through his mischievous activities. ◎ 1025 W Georgia St • Map K3

2 The Jade Canoe
Haida artist Bill Reid's awe-inspiring bronze creation is the second casting of *The Black Canoe*. Thirteen creatures from Haida mythology paddle an imposing 20-ft (6-m) canoe.
◎ Vancouver International Airport • Map A2

The Jade Canoe, by Bill Reid

3 Inukshuk
Made by Alvin Kanak for Expo '86, the granite sculpture is an Inuit welcome figure, a traditional traveler's marker, although much larger than those found in the North. ◎ English Bay Beach • Map G3

4 Carved Doors
The entrance to UBC's Museum of Anthropology (see p34) is itself a work of art. Made of red cedar by four Gitxsan master carvers, the double doors convey a narrative from the Skeena River region. When closed, the images form the shape of a Northwest Coast bent box used for storage as well as burials.

5 Kwakwaka'wakw Totem Pole
This pole at Victoria's Royal British Columbia Museum (see pp24–5) provides a chance to see a powerful modern interpretation of traditional carving by two young Kwakwaka'wakw artists, Jonathan Henderson and Sean Wonnock. The pole features a mythical thunderbird on top of the tail of an orca.

6 Hetux
International travelers alighting at the Vancouver airport are greeted by *Hetux*, a huge birch-and-aluminum image suspended from the ceiling. Connie Watts combines animal forms as diverse as the mythical thunderbird with the hummingbird, wolf, and salmon to reflect the untamed spirit of her grandmother. ◎ Vancouver International Airport • Map A2

7 Thunderbird House Post
Tony Hunt's majestic thunderbird stands above a grizzly bear, which holds a human being. The house post is a replica of one of a pair carved in the early 1900s by influential artist Charlie James. After 40 years in Stanley Park, the poles deteriorated, were restored, and moved indoors. Carver Tony Hunt re-created the colorful pole now standing in the park's Brockton Point Visitor Centre (see p9).

Totem art represents family clans with figures such as eagles, frogs, ravens, orcas, and grizzly bears; mythical creatures are also common

8 Chief of the Undersea World

Orcas were still kept at the Vancouver Aquarium when Haida artist Bill Reid's sculpture was installed outside it, in 1984. Those orcas are since gone, but this 16-ft- (5-m-) tall bronze killer whale leaping into the air remains as a tribute to this West Coast creature. ◊ *Stanley Park • Map G1*

9 World's Tallest Freestanding Totem Pole

Raised in Beacon Hill Park *(see p96)* in 1956, the pole, by Kwakwaka'-wakw chief Mungo Martin with David Martin and Henry Hunt, took six months to carve from a cedar nearly 128 ft (39 m) high. ◊ *Map Q6*

10 Coast Salish Welcome Figures

Two 17-ft- (5-m-) tall red cedar figures welcome travelers to the airport's Custom Hall in traditional Musqueam style. Northwest Coast artist Susan A. Point carved both from the same log. ◊ *Vancouver International Airport • Map A2*

Coast Salish welcome figures

Top 10 Public Artworks

1 A-maze-ing Laughter
Crowds gather around these playful figures. ◊ *Denman and Davie sts • Map G2 & H4*

2 Photo Session
Join Seward Johnson's family of bronze figures posing for a snapshot. ◊ *Queen Elizabeth Park • Map B2*

3 The Crab
George Norris's stylized stainless-steel crab. ◊ *1100 Chestnut St • Map G4*

4 Gate to the Pacific Northwest
Alan Chung Hung's sculpture invokes 18th-century navigation instruments. ◊ *Vanier Park • Map G4*

5 Douglas Coupland's Digital Orca
This piece captures the spirit of Vancouver's harborfront. ◊ *Vancouver Convention and Exhibition Centre • Map L2*

6 Salute to the Lions of Vancouver
Gathie Falk's steel lions line up with the Lions Gate Bridge and The Lions mountain. ◊ *999 Canada Place Way • Map L2*

7 Angel of Victory
Coeur de Lion MacCarthy's bronze angel lifts a World War I soldier heavenward. ◊ *601 W Cordova St • Map L3*

8 Street Light
Panels shadow images of historic events onto a walkway. ◊ *Marinaside Cres • Map K5*

9 Pendulum
A stunning seven-story pendulum, by Alan Storey. ◊ *885 W Georgia St • Map K3*

10 The Inukshuk
This stone statue became BC's emblem during the 2010 Winter Olympics. ◊ *English Bay • Map G2*

Left **Sunken Garden, Butchart Gardens** Right **Macaw parrots, Bloedel Floral Conservatory**

🔟 Parks & Gardens

1 Pacific Spirit Regional Park
This huge, diverse, park is located on a peninsula on Vancouver's west side. It supports pine forests as well as birch, alder, and cottonwood trees. Extensive trails lead across the peninsula from Point Grey to the Fraser River. The park's terrain includes beaches, bluffs overlooking the expansive Spanish Banks, and the ancient Camosun Bog (see p88).

2 David Lam Park
With a large expanse of open green space, the slightly rolling Yaletown park has private corners for sitting and relaxing, and a lovely decorative pool. The park's Asian influence is expressed in its floral plantings. Children's play area. ◈ Map J5

3 Queen Elizabeth Park
This lovely park in central Vancouver was once a stone quarry. The Quarry Garden is now its centerpiece. A small rose garden is planted with hardy varieties that blossom year-round. Rolling treed slopes are perfect for summer picnics (see p88).

4 Stanley Park
Cedar, hemlock, and fir are rainforest favorites in the park. Old-fashioned roses and lush hybrid rhododendrons share the park with cherry, magnolia, and dogwood trees, and a multitude of others. Park staff plant 350,000 annual flowers for year-round beauty (see pp8–11).

5 Bloedel Floral Conservatory
Visitors to Canada's first geodesic conservatory are enveloped by steamy air as they step into this dome filled with desert and tropical plants. The calls of free-flying birds add to the ambience.
◈ Queen Elizabeth Park, W 33rd Ave & Cambie St • Map B2 • 604 257 8584

6 Spanish Banks Beach Park
With the longest expanse of sandy beach in Vancouver, the park is shared by walkers, cyclists, picnickers, and families splashing in the tidal waters. ◈ Map A2

7 Dr. Sun Yat-Sen Classical Chinese Garden
This gem of a park in Chinatown reflects the serenity of a Ming Dynasty garden (see p63).

Dr. Sun Yat-Sen Classical Chinese Garden

Spanish Banks, beside Pacific Spirit Regional Park, is one of the best spots in the city to watch the sun set over the water

Camosun Bog, Pacific Spirit Regional Park

Butchart Gardens
Starting in 1904, Mrs. Jenny Butchart created five spectacular gardens to beautify her huband's excavated limestone quarry on the outskirts of Victoria. Her first creation was the Japanese Garden. Next came the lush Sunken Garden. Some one million bedding plants blossom yearly, showcasing 700 plant varieties *(see p101)*.

VanDusen Botanical Garden
The array of flowers, shrubs, and trees are unrivaled in Vancouver. Over 7,500 varieties of plants from six continents take advantage of the city's four distinct seasons. Rolling lawns, peaceful lakes, artistic rockwork, and forested pockets *(see p88)*.

Vanier Park
English Bay is the backdrop for this expansive park near Granville Island. Largely treeless, the 37-acre (15-ha) area was named after Georges P. Vanier, governor general of Canada from 1959 to 1967. Kite-flyers delight in the open vista, their colorful kites dancing in the wind *(see p78)*.

Top 10 BC Trees

Douglas Fir
The province's economy was built on the lumber from this imposing tree that grows as tall as 300 ft (90 m).

Yellow Cedar
Growing in colder elevations, its soft wood is the ideal choice for First Nations carvings.

Western Red Cedar
Dark, scale-like needles mark the down swept branches of this sometimes huge tree.

Hemlock
The most common tree on the West Coast, the hemlock is easily recognizable by its droopy top.

Sitka Spruce
The Carmanah Giant, a Sitka spruce found on Vancouver Island is, at 312 ft (95 m), the tallest recorded tree in Canada.

Arbutus
Peeling red-brown bark marks the arbutus, also known as the madrona, the only broad-leafed evergreen tree native to Canada.

Pine
Straight lodgepole and Ponderosa pines grow at higher elevations.

Dogwood
The white or pink flowers of the province's floral emblem bloom in spring.

Japanese Flowering Cherry
More than 19,000 of these exquisite blossoming trees line Vancouver city streets.

Maple
Canada's national tree grows in bigleaf, Douglas, and vine varieties. Bigleaf wood is used for First Nations canoe paddles.

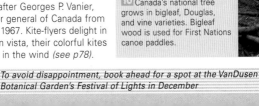

To avoid disappointment, book ahead for a spot at the VanDusen Botanical Garden's Festival of Lights in December

Left **Hawksworth** Right **Wildebeest**

Vancouver & Victoria's Top 10

🔟 Restaurants

1 Hawksworth

Situated in an elegant room at the legendary Rosewood Hotel Georgia, this gem has garnered multiple awards for its dazzling food and star chef David Hawksworth. His 48-hour beef short rib with black pepper jam, shrimp salt, honeydew, and green papaya is the stand-out dish *(see p73)*.

2 CinCin Ristorante & Bar

The Italian-inspired menu of this inviting space includes dishes from the wood-fired oven. If you're not in a rush, order the melt-in-your-mouth free range chicken cooked under a brick in the wood-fired oven for 25 minutes. On the terrace, trees mute the hustle of the street below. Choose from 800 wines *(see p73)*.

CinCin Ristorante & Bar

3 Blue Water Café and Raw Bar

The freshest and finest wild seafood is served in a 100-year-old brick-and-beam warehouse. The decor is contemporary, the atmosphere friendly, and the kitchen serves mouth-watering delicacies such as sablefish in soy and ginger broth, and seafood towers of fresh shellfish, sushi, and Dungeness crab. The Raw Bar is the domain of a master sushi chef. Superb champagne list *(see p83)*.

4 Wildebeest

The 48-hour braised short ribs at this hip Gastown eatery has brought diners to near-delirium. Wildebeest's "farm-house chic" food features unique produce, such as black Spanish radishes and heritage Romano beans, while adventurous meat-eaters are catered for with roasted bone marrow and sweetbreads. Finish with a selection of delicious cheeses from around the world, served with fruit bread, honeyed nuts, and seasonal fruits. *(see p65)*.

5 Bao Bei

On the edge of Chinatown, hipsters and oldsters alike rave about the sliders of lamb sirloin, heavenly dumplings, and innovative small plates at this Chinese brasserie. This restaurant does not take reservations so it is best to arrive early. With advance notice, groups of 8 to 12 diners can enjoy a tasting menu at the large family table *(see p91)*.

Blue Water Café and Raw Bar

West Coast cuisine highlights local seafood, meats, and produce, often incorporating ingredients unique to the region

Diva at the Met

Diva at the Met
Chef Hamid Salimian is a master of molecular gastronomy, serving up innovative cuisine from Diva's open kitchen. His unique offerings include puffed *foie gras* in caramelized fig dotted with candied walnuts and pickled green strawberries. A sommelier helps choose from 550 wines (see p73).

Chambar
Success hasn't spoilt this Belgian restaurant in the Crosstown neighborhood. It is one of the hottest eateries in town and perenially packed. Traditional dishes such as *moules frites* excel, but for a real treat try the *Congolaise* version, where mussels are cooked in a tomato and coconut cream sauce with smoked chili and lime (see p65).

Raincity Grill
White tablecloths, leather banquets, and wood floors, combine with killer views over English Bay, creating casual yet upscale dining. The menu is organic and seasonal: game in winter gives way to fish choices in summer (see p73).

Cioppino's Mediterranean Grill
Inventive *cucina*-style dishes are made with fresh vegetables, olive oil, and low-fat cream sauces for a pleasing meal that is easy on the waistline. Or choose the juicy Black Angus beef with calamari, lobster, and escargot. A patio and excellent wine list round out the experience (see p83).

C Restaurant
This sleek waterfront eatery is devoted to serving sustainable seafood and ingredients that are distinctive and homegrown – try the divine Qualicum Bay scallops or the seared BC albacore tuna. C is the founding restaurant in the Vancouver Aquarium Ocean Wise Program (see p83).

Early-bird **prix fixe** menus offer economy and variety at some restaurants; call ahead for details

Left **Queen Elizabeth Theatre & Vancouver Playhouse** Right **BC Place**

TOP 10 Entertainment Venues

1 Queen Elizabeth Theatre & Vancouver Playhouse

Home to the Vancouver Opera and Ballet BC, and hosting many guest artists, the Queen Elizabeth Theatre is located in a 1960s-built, Modernist venue. Adjacent to it, in an urbane yet cozy space, the Vancouver Playhouse Theatre Company hosts the Friends of Chamber Music, DanceHouse, and the Vancouver Recital Society. ✆ *Hamilton at Dunsmuir sts • Map L4 • 604 665 3050 • www.city.vancouver. bc.ca/theatres*

2 Commodore Ballroom

The Commodore has been around for more than 75 years. Its eclectic national and international acts have included Talking Heads, Tina Turner, and Dizzy Gillespie, as well as Canada's hottest bands and solo artists, and world music performers. Tickets required *(see p74).*

The Fabulous
COMMODORE
Ballroom

Commodore Ballroom sign

3 Stanley Industrial Alliance Stage

This 1930s movie house was restored to its former elegance in the 1990s. It is now home to the Arts Club Theatre Company's classic and contemporary dramas, comedies, and musicals. The Stanley is one of the city's most nostalgic venues, remembered fondly by many oldtimers. ✆ *2750 Granville St • Map B2 • 604 687 1644 • www.artsclub.com*

4 Rogers Arena

This huge venue is home to the Vancouver Canucks National Hockey League team. The arena is also one of the busiest entertainment venues in North America: since 1995, the venue has hosted some 170 concerts and events each year. ✆ *Pacific Blvd N at Abbott St • Map L4 • 604 899 7889 • www.rogersarena.ca*

5 BC Place

A Vancouver landmark, this stadium opened in 1983. Its covering, which is now retractable, is the largest air-supported roof in the world. Football is the main attraction, featuring the BC Lions, as well as major concerts and trade shows. The stadium converts in a few hours from a 60,000-seat football field to a 30,000-seat concert bowl. ✆ *777 Pacific Blvd • Map L4–L5 • 604 669 2300 • www.bcplace.com*

6 Vancouver East Cultural Centre

Canadian and international theater and dance, as well as local and world music, are all presented in this renovated 1909 Methodist church, which now has a studio stage. The "Cultch" is one of the first LEED (Leadership in Energy and Environmental Design) certified arts centers in Canada. ✆ *1895 Venables St • Map B2 • 604 251 1363 • www.thecultch.com*

*For events listings, check out **The Georgia Straight**, a free weekly Vancouver tabloid See p110*

The Orpheum

7 Restored to Baroque grandeur, the Orpheum is a lush, former Vaudeville palace built in 1926. Vancouver-born Hollywood star Yvonne de Carlo was an usherette here briefly in the late 1930s. Vancouver Symphony Orchestra and choral concerts, rock shows, and other quality musical events are performed here in the acoustically upgraded space. ◈ 884 Granville St • Map K4 • 604 665 3050 • www.vancouver.ca/theatres

Firehall Arts Centre

8 This heritage fire station, circa 1906, is now an innovative Gastown theater. Modern plays, many by home-grown talents, reflect cultural diversity through comedy and drama. The 175-seat studio theater includes an outdoor stage. A cozy, licensed lounge offers a chance to mix with local theater-goers. ◈ 280 E Cordova St • Map M4 • 604 689 0926 • www.firehallartscentre.ca

Granville Island Stage/Revue Stage

9 The Arts Club Theatre Company's 440-seat Granville Island Stage and its more intimate 198-seat Revue Stage, prove theatre doesn't have to be formal.

The Orpheum

New and classic comedies, dramas, and musicals are featured at both venues. ◈ Granville Island Stage: 1585 Johnston St, 604 687 1644; Revue Stage, 1601 Johnston St, 604 687 1644 • Map H5 • www.artsclub.com

Chan Centre for the Performing Arts

10 In this striking, cylindrical, three-venue center music is performed in the glorious 1,200-seat Chan Shun Concert Hall, whose adjustable acoustic canopy allows all types of music to sound their best. A small, experimental theater and a cinema round out the entertainment venues. ◈ 6265 Crescent Rd, University of British Columbia • Map A2 • 604 822 9197 • www.chancentre.com

Left **Bard on the Beach** Right **Vancouver Pride Festival parade**

Festivals & Events

1 Bard on the Beach Shakespeare Festival

Bard on the Beach, Western Canada's largest professional Shakespeare festival, presents works by the Bard, and related events. English Bay forms the backdrop for the open-air stages. *Vanier Park • Map G4 • Jun–late Sep • 604 739 0559*

2 Alcan Canadian International Dragon Boat Festival

Over 2,500 paddlers from around the world gather for a weekend of exhilarating fun. There's more to do than just watch the races. Food, exhibits, and entertainment abound. Admission to Science World is included in the ticket price. *False Creek • mid-Jun • 604 688 2382*

Alcan Dragon Boat Festival

3 Honda Celebration of Light

The night skies fill with spectacular fireworks, accompanied by broadcasted music, as three countries compete to win top bragging rights. Huge crowds flock to English Bay, Vanier Park, Kitsilano, Jericho, and West Vancouver beaches, so go early to snag a good spot, and bring a blanket to sit on. *Jul & Aug*

4 Vancouver Pride Festival

For two weeks, gays and friends of gays gather in the city's West End to celebrate diversity. The festival is a bevy of picnics, dances, cruises, breakfasts, and a grand finale parade and beachside party, with thousands in attendance. *late Jul–early Aug • 604 687 0955*

5 Vancouver International Wine Festival

From humble beginnings in 1979, the VanWineFest hosts premier industry names and is considered to be one of the biggest, best, and oldest wine events in the world. It features wine tastings and pairings, gourmet dinners and luncheons, educational seminars, and culinary competitions. *late Feb–early Mar • 604 873 3311*

Fireworks, Honda Celebration of Light

For tickets to many of Vancouver's events and festivals, contact Ticketmaster 604 280 4444, www.ticketmaster.ca

6 Vancouver International Film Festival

Eclectic yet accessible programming draws more than 150,000 people to the city's annual film festival, which includes a strong showing of films from Canada and the Pacific Rim. ✆ *early Oct* • *604 685 0260*

7 Vancouver International Jazz Festival

Jazz in every imaginable style and all its dimensions, from upwardly mobile performers to big names, is presented in some 400 concerts at various venues around town. Wraps up with an outdoor multi-stage free weekend.
✆ *late Jun–early Jul* • *604 872 5200*

8 Vancouver Writers Fest

International and Canadian writers attract throngs of readers to forums, readings, and literary cabarets in English and French. Writers stay on the festival site, so there's a good chance you'll see and even chat to a celebrity author. ✆ *Granville Island* • *late Oct* • *604 681 6330*

9 Vancouver Folk Music Festival

Canadian and international performers play rain or shine in open-air stages. The waterside park becomes its own township as 30,000 folk music fanatics settle in for three evenings and two full days of non-stop music and good vibrations. ✆ *Jericho Beach Park* • *mid-Jul* • *604 602 9798*

10 Vancouver International Comedy Festival

Generous doses of stand-up, burlesque, sketch comedy, improvisation, and free street performances by top Canadian and international comedians.
✆ *mid-Oct* • *604 685 0881*

Top 10 Performing Groups

1 Firehall Arts Centre
Entertaining shows with a multi-cultural twist *(see p43)*.

2 Ballet British Columbia
World-class ballet under bold leadership. ✆ *Ticketmaster: 1-855-985-5000.*

3 Vancouver Recital Society
The VRS has a reputation for innovation and excellence in programming. ✆ *604 873 3311*

4 Vancouver Opera Company
Grand-scale productions of traditional and contemporary pieces. ✆ *604 683 0222*

5 Vancouver Symphony Orchestra
World-class orchestral music, often with international guest artists. ✆ *Ticketmaster: 1-855-985-5000.*

6 Early Music Vancouver
Varied concerts of works by Medieval to late-Romantic composers. ✆ *604 732 1610*

7 Arts Club Theatre Company
Contemporary drama at Granville Island Stage and the Stanley Theatre. ✆ *Ticketmaster: 1-855-985-5000.*

8 Vancouver Theatresports League
Hilarious improv-based comedy and parody at Granville Island's Improv Centre. ✆ *604 738 7013*

9 Kokoro Dance Company
Distorted movement and great intensity characterize Kokoro's *butoh*, a postwar Japanese dance form. ✆ *604 662 7441*

10 Hoarse Raven Theatre
This ambitious small company has garnered many awards. ✆ *604 608 6799*

Left **Science World** Right **Sea otter, Vancouver Aquarium**

Children's Attractions

1 Science World
Kids can get involved in the displays at this hands-on discovery center and they won't even know they're learning something. A good rainy day diversion, Science World also has healthy fast-food dining *(see pp22–3)*.

2 Stanley Park
Stanley Park's miniature railway makes a 15-minute excursion through the forest. Kids can get up close to goats, sheep, pigs, and other animals at the Children's Farmyard, or take a splash in the waterpark near Lumberman's Arch.

Miniature Railway, Stanley Park

There's plenty to do for free, too. Second Beach has a play area, swimming pool, and beach. *Stanley Park • Map G1 • 604 257 8531 (railway) • Open year-round; hours vary • Adm • www.parks.vancouver.bc.ca*

3 Capilano Suspension Bridge Park
Walk the swaying bridge, then climb Treetops Adventure's boardwalks and platforms perched high in the forest *(see pp14–15)*.

4 OMNIMAX® Theatre
Kids will feel like they're in the middle of the action when watching films on the five-story screen situated in the Science World building *(see p22)*.

5 Vancouver Aquarium
Canada's largest aquarium introduces kids to everything from eels and octopuses to tropical fish in re-created natural habitats. Naturalists are on hand to answer questions. Special events for kids include sleepovers with the Beluga whales *(see pp10–11)*.

6 Granville Island Water Park
On a hot summer day kids will love splashing in the cool spray, shooting water cannons, and zooming down two separate water slides at this large water park. There is a small playground nearby, and bathrooms and changing rooms in the False Creek Community Centre next door. Best of all, it's free. *1318 Cartwright St • Map H5/6 • 604 257 8195 • Open summer only (check website for opening hours) • www.falsecreekcc.ca*

Capilano Suspension Bridge Park

OMNIMAX® Theatre showings range from nature documentaries to animated features to remastered Hollywood blockbusters

Skyride, Grouse Mountain

7 Grouse Mountain
Grouse offers more than just skiing and snowboarding. Summer activities include hiking, ziplining, paragliding, guided eco-walks, or riding the Skyride to the top. At the Refuge for Endangered Wildlife, see peregrine falcons, gray wolves, and grizzlies. Loggers throw axes and roll logs at the lumberjack show *(see p86)*.

8 H.R. MacMillan Space Centre
Touch a moon rock, morph into an alien, or climb aboard a spacecraft and let the motion simulator replicate the feeling of space travel. Laser and star shows *(see p78)*.

9 Playland & the Pacific National Exhibition
Playland has rides for all ages, including its famed wooden roller coaster, plus a climbing wall, mini-golf, midway games, and cotton candy. The Pacific National Exhibition runs mid-August to September, with animals, entertainment, and demolition derbies. Ⓢ *2901 E Hastings St • Map B2 • 604 253 2311 • Open Jun–Sep: daily; Apr–May: Sat & Sun; hrs vary • Adm • www.pne.ca*

10 Maplewood Farm
Kids enjoy pony rides, sheep shearing, cow milking, and mingling with the animals at this farm. Picnic area, greenhouse, and aviary, too. Ⓢ *405 Seymour River Pl, N Vancouver • Map C1 • 604 929 5610*

Top 10 Places to Eat with Kids

1 Old Spaghetti Factory
Pastas and more in a memorabilia-filled warehouse. Ⓢ *53 Water St • 604 684 1288*

2 White Spot
Classic burgers, fries, and Pirate Packs, as well as healthier choices. Ⓢ *580 W Georgia St • 604 681 8034*

3 Sophie's Cosmic Café
Fun 1950s decor with booths, big portions of comfort food, weekend lineups. Ⓢ *2095 W 4th Ave • 604 732 6810*

4 Sha Lin Noodle House
Cheap and yummy noodles, made before your eyes. Ⓢ *656 W Broadway • 604 873 1618*

5 Café Deux Soleil
Where hip young vegetarian families meet. Toddlers' play area. Ⓢ *2096 Commercial Dr • 604 254 1195*

6 Cat's Social House
Unfussy lunch spot near Granville Island's Kids Market. Ⓢ *1540 Old Bridge St • 604 647 2287*

7 Little Nest
Kid- and parent-friendly dining with delicious get-healthy options. Ⓢ *1716 Charles St • 604 251 9994*

8 Earl's
Dishes for everyone, from pizza to fine dinners. Ⓢ *1185 Robson St • 604 669 0020*

9 Boathouse
Relaxed West Coast cuisine, children's menu, great view from the patio. Ⓢ *1795 Beach Ave • 604 669 2225*

10 Topanga Café
A laid-back Vancouver favorite serving California-style Mexican food from a menu that children can have fun coloring. Ⓢ *2904 W 4th Ave • 604 733 3713*

Several of the kids-friendly restaurants listed have multiple locations; check the phone book

Left **Seawall, English Bay** Right **Snowboarder, Cypress Provincial Park**

Great Outdoor Places

English Bay

1 This beautiful bay is a popular West End attraction. On New Year's Day it hosts the polar bear swim, when thousands of swimmers brave the cold waters. More popular is walking the seawall that runs beside the bay into Stanley Park, fueled with caffeine or ice cream from nearby Davie and Denman street cafés *(see p8)*.

Lighthouse Park

2 Park in the convenient lot or hop off the bus and enjoy a fairly easy walk though West Vancouver's 500-year-old forest to the boulder-lined shore, and the 1912 Point Atkinson Light-

Lighthouse, Lighthouse Park

house. The old-growth forest was slated to be felled to provide fuel for the lighthouse and its steam fog alarm. Luckily, it was never logged. Six miles (9.5 km) of trails provide day hikes through this entirely natural park, with its native trees and plants *(see p88)*.

Jericho Beach

3 This family-friendly park has an outdoor shower and changing rooms for freshening up after a day splashing in the water. Picnics on the beach are a favorite pastime. To take advantage of Pacific breezes, rent a windsurfer. Lessons are available for beginners to advanced. ◈ *Map A1 • Windsure Windsurfing: 604 224 0615*

Cypress Provincial Park

4 Cypress Mountain, one of the park's several peaks, is the biggest alpine ski and snowboarding area on the North Shore. In summer, activities include mountain biking, hiking, and wilderness camping in the park's rugged backcountry areas. ◈ *Map A1 • 604 926 5612*

Grouse Mountain

5 The gondola ride to the summit provides thrilling views of the city and beyond. Skiing and snowboarding are guaranteed in winter, courtesy of snowmakers. Sightseeing and lots of activities in the summer *(see p86)*.

Kitsilano Beach and Park

6 "Kits" Park is connected by a tree-lined walk to the beach, favored by swimsuit-clad volleyball players and sunbathers. Busy Olympic-size Kitsilano Pool overlooks the beach. ◈ *Map B2 • Kitsilano Pool: 311*

Kitsilano Beach

A seawalk extends from west of Jericho Beach through Kitsilano and Vanier parks (see p78) to Granville Island (see pp20–21) and beyond

7 Wreck Beach

Getting down to Wreck Beach is easy, via a steep trail leading from SW Marine Drive on the UBC campus (see p85). The hard part is the climb back up from this clothing-optional beach. Beware: ogglers on the beach are conspicuous. There are spectacular views across the Strait of Georgia toward Vancouver Island (see p53).

8 Mount Seymour Provincial Park

Drive to the top of Mount Seymour for glimpses of deer and bears, and for views of Deep Cove and Indian Arm. The park, on the eastern end of the Coast Mountain range, is popular in winter, with gentle slopes for beginners as well as challenges for more advanced skiers and snowboarders. Hiking is a summer activity. The park encompasses Mount Seymour, Mount Elsay, and Mount Bishop. ◐ Map C1 • 604 986 2261

9 Beacon Hill Park

Since 1858, Beacon Hill Park has been the queen of Victoria's open-air spaces. Wooden bridges over the stream, petting zoo, and English-style rose garden add charm to the peaceful setting. Views of the Strait of Juan de Fuca from some points in the 62-acre (25-ha) park. Visitors can walk, bird-watch, ride horses, and picnic on the beach (see p96).

10 Cathedral Grove

The grove, located in MacMillan Provincial Park on Vancouver Island, provides an awe-inspiring look at a virgin coastal forest. Giant, ancient Douglas-fir trees share the forest with stands of hemlock and Western red cedar. Loop trails are located on either side of Hwy 4. Scenic Cameron Lake is nearby. ◐ Map C4

Top 10 Outdoor Activities

1 Cycling

Stanley Park's seawall (see p8) has a dedicated bike lane. ◐ Spokes Bicycle Rentals, 1798 W Georgia St • 604 688 5141

2 Sailing

English Bay and Vancouver's outer harbor beckon. ◐ Simplicity Sailing Charters • 604 765 0074

3 Rock Climbing

Over 1,000 routes on the Squamish Chief make it a top climbing destination (see p89).

4 Skiing & Snowboarding

Whistler-Blackcomb is one of the top resorts in North America (see pp28–31).

5 Hiking

Completing the 2-mile (3-km) Grouse Grind wins you bragging rights (see p86).

6 Canoeing & Kayaking

Vancouver and Gulf Island canoeing and kayaking take little training. ◐ Lotus Land Tours • 604 684 4922

7 Golfing

Golden Ears mountains are the backdrop for a championship course. ◐ Newlands Golf & Country Club, 21025 48th Ave, Langley • 604 533 3288

8 In-line Skating

Stanley Park's seawall (see p8) makes for a satisfyingly long skate. ◐ Bayshore Rentals, 745 Denman St • 604 688 2453

9 Snowshoeing

Take a few minutes to master the skill, then enjoy the pristine wilderness. ◐ Cypress Mountain • 604 926 5612

10 Whale-Watching

Don a sweater and waterproof jacket, bring your binoculars, and watch the majestic orcas (see p109).

Left **AuBAR** Right **Vancouver FanClub**

Bars & Clubs

AuBAR Nightclub

An upscale feel is created by the polished decor, complete with candles dotting the tables of the intimate seating areas. Lofty 22-ft (7-m) ceilings give an open feel to the dance floor. Friday night features top DJs spinning hip-hop and R&B, while Saturday nights percolate with Top 40s music. Plush seating in the lounge is also inviting. High-rollers drink Courvoisier and Hennessey. Fruity martinis such as Carmel Apple, Passion, and Starburst are favorites. This is definitely a see-and-be-seen type of place. You might even spot a Hollywood celebrity or two in the crowd. Dress code enforced *(see p74)*.

ginger 62

The action in this self-styled "cocktail den and kitchen" starts at 8pm every night of the week. The atmosphere of the bar, with its dance floor, lounge, and more intimate Red Room, is a mix of 1960s and Asian inspirations. Reservations are a must for a seat at the cool white-and-red banquets. Live music and hot DJs – spinning hip-hop, R&B, club tracks, house, and more – are boosted by tasty Asian-influenced tapas. Delicious martinis and cocktails such as Frank & Dean and Ginger Not Marianne, are favourites with the hip crowd. *(see p74)*.

ginger 62 sign

Vancouver FanClub

At this one-stop shop for live entertainment, dancing, and dining, guests can boogie to the rhythm of live blues, funk, or soul on the mezzanine dance floor. If all that dancing makes you hungry, tuck into an eclectic menu of New Orleans-inspired dishes. Drinks included craft beers, wine on tap, customized cocktails, and in-house smoked Bulleit Bourbon *(see p82)*.

Venue

In the heart of the Granville Street club district, Venue boasts a 12,000 sq ft (1,115 sq m), two-level room with a glam-rock inspired interior. Weeknights feature live shows, while on the weekend the city's top alternative DJs spin pop, rock, and retro originals, along with bass-heavy electro mixes *(see p82)*.

Commodore Ballroom

Opened in 1926, this club has weathered many musical eras. Catch one of the many great acts and test out the room's bouncy sprung floor as you dance or party at one of the ample tables along the sides. Updated, and always on the cutting edge of music, the Commodore Ballrooom lives on as the city's great-grandfather of clubs *(see p74)*.

The 12-route NightBus service runs every 30 minutes nightly to 3am; route info: TransLink, 604 953 3333 or www.translink.ca

6 Five Sixty

The latest incarnation of the legendary Richard's on Richards, Five Sixty is a massive club spread over four floors. Several separate lounges, galleries, and bars display local and international artworks and cater to a diverse clientele. There's live music during the week, while DJs pump out the sounds at the weekend. ◈ 560 Seymour St • Map K4 • 604 678 6322

The Irish Heather

7 Caprice Nightclub & Lounge

Clean, lean, and modern, this cavernous nightclub has a dance floor for 400. The music is eclectic, with dee-jayed retro classics and R&B. All-request Top 40 is featured on alternating nights. The lounge, with a separate entrance, is a more intimate space, with its warming fireplace (see p74).

8 The Roxy

A Vancouver institution, The Roxy hosts top Canadian and local bands and is a favorite nightspot of Vancouver Canuck's hockey team. Line-ups at this popular club are common after 9pm, so be warned and get in line early (see p74).

9 The Irish Heather

This gastro-pub serves up good food, including many pub favorites, in a casual and friendly setting. Shebeen, a whiskey house offering a great selection of about 100 single malts, bourbon, rye, scotch, and whiskey, is located in this building (see p64).

10 Celebrities

A legendary Vancouver nightspot in the heart of Davie Village. Although officially categorized as a gay bar, Celebrities is popular across the spectrum and is simply a great place to dance. Music styles vary across the week and include hip-hop, R&B, funk, rock, retro, and house. ◈ 1022 Davie St • Map J4 • 604 681 6180

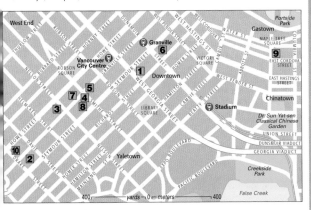

Buy tickets at the door, or at Ticketmaster outlets or online at www.ticketmaster.ca; call 604 280 4444 to charge by phone

51

Left **Patio, Fountainhead Pub** Right **Little Sister's sign**

🔟 Gay & Lesbian Hangouts

1 The Davie Village

Davie Village, with its fuchsia bus shelters and trash bins, is Vancouver's gay 'hood. Located in the West End between Burrard and Jervis streets, it's a 24-hour strip with cafés, myriad shops, including sex shops, clubs, restaurants for all budgets, and bars. The Centre, at 1170 Bute Street, provides health and social services to the community. ✎ Map H4

Davie Village street banners

2 Fountainhead Pub

With its excellent selection of lagers on tap and appetizing menu, the Fountainhead Pub is a good first stop when hitting Davie Village. As a neighborhood sports bar, it's a great place to watch sports play-offs on TV. The patio is a prime spot for people-watching in the thick of the Village. ✎ 1025 Davie St • Map J4 • 604 687 2222

3 Little Sister's Book & Art Emporium

If there is an anchor to Vancouver's gay community, Little Sister's is it. More than a bookstore, it's a long-standing institution that has taken Canada Customs to the Supreme Court of Canada in its fight for freedom from censorship. Good selection of literature, event tickets, gift items, clothing, DVDs, and play things. ✎ 1238 Davie St • Map H3 • 604 669 1753

4 Man Up

Man Up is an ongoing series of events centred around a monthly showcase of drag king performances. Check the website www.manupvancouver.com for upcoming events and ticket information. ✎ 917 Main St • Map M4 • 604 992 4352

5 Sunset Beach

Adorned with Pride flags in the summer, Sunset Beach along English Bay is the destination for those with coffees-to-go from nearby cafés. Grab a park bench or a spot on the sandy beach and watch the world go by. Or enjoy the vista from one of the bars and restaurants along the waterfront. In the heat of summer, the beach sizzles with skin and buff bods. It's also a great place to swim and suntan (see p48).

Sunset Beach

The Centre provides referrals, counseling, a library, and various programs; call 604 684 5307 or visit www.qmunity.ca

Celebrities

Celebrities
Brilliant lighting and visuals, state-of-the-art sound, and the city's hottest DJs and performers get the crowd – gay, straight, bi, and curious – moving. ⊗ *1022 Davie St • Map J4 • 604 681 6180*

Delaney's Coffee House
Perhaps the city's most popular see-and-be-seen coffee house, with a good-sized patio. ⊗ *1105 Denman St • Map G2 • 604 662 3344*

Wreck Beach
Beneath the cliffs of Point Grey and accessible by steep trails through the rainforest, Wreck Beach is a must for those who enjoy sunbathing *au natural*. Vendors sell everything from piña coladas to tanning oil. ⊗ *Map A1*

1181
This sophisticated queer lounge and bar describes itself as "a mix of cork and mirror that capture headlight glare from cars cruising Davie Street". ⊗ *1181 Davie St • Map J4 • 604 787 7130*

Numbers Cabaret
This fun, friendly, and unpretentious gay club is usually packed with people from all walks of life. There's something for everyone, including pool tables, darts, DJs pumping out sounds across five dancefloors, and Karaoke Funbox in the loft every night. Ongoing events include cabaret nights and drag shows. Daily drinks specials feature cocktails and jugs of beer. ⊗ *1042 Davie St • Map J4 • 604 685 4077*

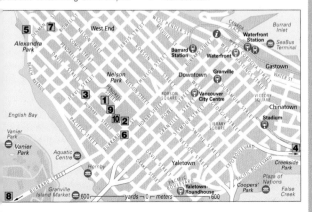

While the West End is extremely gay-friendly, care should be taken when visiting Stanley Park at night

Left **Fashions, Robson Street** Right **Italian boots at Bionic Footwear, South Granville**

🔟 Shopping Destinations

1 Robson Street
Fashionable Robson Street's shopping epicenter is the corner of Burrard and Robson where Virgin Megastore and Roots Canada (see p72) make their homes. Browse internationally known clothing, shoe, accessory, and home furnishing stores, or shop for clothing at Canadian-owned Aritzia. Try Lush for bath and body products. Take a breather at any of the many restaurants en route (see p69).

2 Granville Island
There's more to shopping on the Island than just fresh foods at the Public Market: look for silver jewelry and hats among the stalls (see p80). The Net Loft – once used for fishing net repairs – sells neat things, such as handmade paper and hand-dyed clothing. The bountiful Kids Market offers lots of minishops and activities for the wee ones (see pp20–21). **Pousse café glassware, Granville Island**

3 Gastown
Gastown's century-old buildings have morphed into one-of-a-kind boutiques, First Nations art galleries, and specialty shops selling everything from buttons to cowboy boots to urban designer clothing. Gastown has long been known for souvenirs, and many retailers selling both classic and kitsch Canadiana line Water Street and the smaller streets leading out from it (see p61).

4 South Granville
South Granville shopping extends along Granville Street from 2nd to 16th avenues. At least a dozen art galleries are found here. The casually elegant strip is home to brand-name and high-end European clothing purveyors such as Bacci, Boboli (see p81), and MaxMara. Fabulous yet affordable footwear awaits at Bionic Footwear and Freedman Shoes. Several lingerie shops, too. ◈ Map H6

5 Sinclair Centre
Four heritage buildings are grouped to create an elegant, upscale shopping mall. The three levels of retail indulgence include two floors of exclusive shops offering luxury accessories and clothing from the likes of Versace, Armani, Prada, and DKNY. The lower level has a food fair. ◈ 757 W Hastings • Map L3

6 Chinatown
Vancouver's oldest and largest ethnic shopping area has struggled at times to survive with competition from Richmond's Asian super-malls. Yet Chinatown hangs on, its crowded streets filled with bargain-hunters. Shops selling herbs and potions, exotic delicacies, fresh seafood and vegetables, leather goods, and Asian souvenirs appear elbow to elbow (see p62).

Shopabout Tours, run by knowledgeable locals, hits the city's retail hot spots; call 604 375 1228 or visit www.shopabout.ca

Metrotown

Metropolis at Metrotown is BC's largest mall. The atmosphere is charged with the energy of thousands of daily shoppers. Department stores The Bay and Sears (see p112) anchor the mall, with chains and independents well represented by 470 stores. The 17 movie theaters and three games centers ensure that there's entertainment for all, even if shopping's not their thing. ❂ 4720 Kingsway, Burnaby • Map C2 • 604 438 4700

Pacific Centre

More than 150 stores and services stretch beneath Granville Street in the heart of downtown Vancouver. After checking out The Bay, a major department store among the many street-level shops, descend to the boutiques and specialty stores below, selling clothing, jewelry, sportswear, gadgets, and more. High-end retailers include Holt Renfrew (see p70).

Broadway

Originally designed to be the city's major thoroughfare, Broadway's shopping hotspots are located between Main and Alma streets. Mountain Equipment Co-op, at the eastern end, requires a small membership fee, but the sportswear is superb. Going west, the street is dotted with clothing stores, bookshops, and health food stores, particularly at Granville, Arbutus, and Macdonald streets, the latter home to the city's Greektown. ❂ Map A1–B1

Clothing store, Commercial Drive

Commercial Drive

The Drive, as it's known locally, is funky and fun, the epitome of hip and casual. Once Vancouver's Little Italy, the area is now an easy-going, multi-ethnic mix of clothing shops, book and magazine stores, vintage-wear boutiques, and second-hand outlets. Start at East Broadway and Commercial Drive and walk north to Venables Street, admiring the distant Coast Mountains along the way. ❂ Map B2

Metropolis at Metrotown has over 4,000 spaces in its free parking lot, or access the mall via SkyTrain, alighting at Metrotown station

55

Left **Vida** Right **A massage at Grotto Spa**

Spas

Willow Stream Spa
The signature treatment, Island Senses for Healthy Energy, includes a pine hydrotherapy bath and restoring massage with aromatic lavender oil. The spa's setting is as romantic as the hotel it's located in. ✆ *Fairmont Empress Hotel, 721 Government St, Victoria* • *Map P4* • *250 995 4650*

Vida
Clients are first analyzed by specialists in Ayurvedic massage for the best way to treat their *dosha*, or body composition, using 5,000-year-old holistic techniques. Then it's on to balancing the *dosha* with dry brushing, a steam in the cedar cabinet, and essential oil massages. ✆ *Fairmont Chateau Whistler* • *Map F1* • *604 938 2086*

Essential oils

Spa at the Wedgewood
A full-service hotel spa offering the Chai Soy anti-stress back treatment, which also includes a relaxing scalp and foot massage. The cinnamon enzyme facial, with its skin tightening effect, is a favorite. ✆ *845 Hornby St* • *Map K3* • *604 689 7777*

Grotto Spa
Overlooking an expanse of beach, BC's largest spa resort offers a wide range of treatments, including couple's massages. West Coast seaweed is part of a sensuous scrub, wrap, facial, and massage package. ✆ *Tigh-Na-Mara Seaside Resort and Spa, 1155 Resort Dr, Parksville* • *Map C4* • *250 248 2072*

Absolute Spa at the Century
Escape into relaxation at this gloriously refurbished spa. Choose ancient Moor Mud to whisk away impurities, signature facial treatments, or a luscious milk bath, just as Cleopatra enjoyed. Organic grapefruit treatments for hands, feet, and body. ✆ *Century Plaza Hotel, 1015 Burrard St* • *Map J4* • *604 684 2772*

Spa Utopia
Awaken your senses with a signature facial that uses hot stones and Japanese facial techniques or experience full-body benefits with an Amazon berry wrap. ✆ *1001–999 Canada Place* • *Map K2* • *604 641 1351*

Silk Road Spa
This spa takes its cue from the Orient, where tea and relaxation balance each other for harmonious effect. Green tea, an antioxidant, is used in some treatments; aromatherapy enhances others. Products are all naturally sourced. ✆ *1624 Government St, Victoria* • *Map P1* • *250 704 2688*

BC has the highest standard in Canada for registered massage therapists (RMT); facilities employing RMTs display certification

Spa at Four Seasons Resort Whistler

8 Spa at Four Seasons Resort Whistler

Eucalyptus steam rooms at this sparkling, high-ceilinged spa offer total relaxation. The BC glacial clay wrap uses rockweed and ocean mud. ⬙ *4591 Blackcomb Way, Whistler • Map F1 • 604 966 2620*

9 skoah

Skin care is the focus at this luxurious spa. Its personalized Facilicious treatment is the most requested. Skin-calming plant extracts are mixed by a staff chemist. ⬙ *1011 Hamilton St • Map J5 • 604 642 0200*

10 Avello Spa & Health Club

This elegant spa specializes in rock- and hydrotherapy. Water jets eliminate toxins; warm stones create trails of relaxing heat on the body. ⬙ *Westin Resort, 4090 Whistler Way, Whistler • Map F1 • 604 935 3444*

Avello Spa & Health Club

Top 10 Health and Body Treatments

1 Hot Stone Massage
Locally sourced lava rocks are heated and applied to the body to eliminate stress and restore energy.

2 Seaweed Wraps
West Coast seaweed mud remineralizes the body. Followed by an application of hot towels, a wrap makes for wonderfully soft skin all over.

3 Plant Extracts Facial
Plants such as refreshing cucumber are blended with extracts, including gingko biloba and St. John's Wort, in creams that make the skin glow.

4 Couple's Massage
Sessions for couples focus on full-body relaxation massage with two therapists.

5 Body Lufa Exfoliation
Organic lufa ground into a fine dust and essential oils are massaged into the skin to hydrate and improve circulation.

6 Ayurvedic Steam Cabinet
A steam in a cedar cabinet is an aromatic way to detoxify.

7 Aromatherapy
Aromatic oils are blended for their mental and physical effects, often with a hint of cedar, pine, or lavender.

8 Spray Tan
Hydrating, nourishing products are used to apply even, sun-free color.

9 Therapeutic Body Massage
This massage combines deep compressions with yoga-like stretches for energy and calm.

10 White Grapefruit Treatment
Detox massage with organic essential oils firms, tones, and hydrates the skin.

Following pages **Entrance, Marine Heritage Building, Vancouver**

AROUND TOWN

VANCOUVER & VICTORIA'S TOP 10

Left **Waterfront Station** Right **Sidewalk stalls, Chinatown**

Waterfront, Gastown & Chinatown

THE WATERFRONT IS VANCOUVER'S HEART. *After New York, the city is North America's second largest port in both size and tonnage. With the opening of the cruise ship terminal at Canada Place in the mid-1980s, it also became one of the world's major cruise ship ports. A block away, Gastown's origin as a tough mill town is masked by gracefully restored heritage buildings constructed during the boom years of the early 1900s. The Landing, next to Waterfront Station, was one of the first to be renovated. Farther along West Cordova Street begins Chinatown, the largest in North America after San Francisco's. The area that was once a marsh is now home to over 35,000 people of Chinese descent, though its growth and prosperity did not come easily – it was seen as a threat by seasonal workers, and a closed-door immigration policy was imposed in 1885. Today, Chinatown attracts throngs of shoppers looking for authentic Chinese food and souvenirs.*

Gassy Jack statue, Gastown

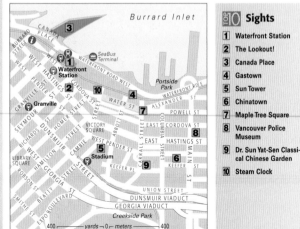

Sights

1. Waterfront Station
2. The Lookout!
3. Canada Place
4. Gastown
5. Sun Tower
6. Chinatown
7. Maple Tree Square
8. Vancouver Police Museum
9. Dr. Sun Yat-Sen Classical Chinese Garden
10. Steam Clock

When you buy a ticket to The Lookout! it is valid for the entire day, so you can easily return for a sunset or night view of Vancouver

Waterfront Station

The station has been a transportation hub since 1887, when the original timber structure welcomed the first cross-Canada passenger train. The present building was built in 1914. With Vancouver Harbour as backdrop, the station's white-columned façade is impressive in a showy way. Inside, murals on the upper walls depict Canadian landscapes. ❧ 601 W Cordova St • Map L3

The Lookout!

The showstopper of the Harbour Centre complex is its 581-ft (177-m) tower, home to The Lookout! observation deck. The ride up in the glass-fronted elevator takes a thrilling 50 seconds. From the enclosed viewing deck, the 360-degree view is splendid. On a clear day, you can see Vancouver Island to the west and Washington State's Mount Baker to the south. In the evening, many return to admire the intense sunsets over the water. ❧ 555 W Hastings St • Map L3 • 604 689 0421 • Open May–Oct: 8:30am–10:30pm; Nov–Apr: 9am–9pm • Adm

Five sails, Canada Place

Canada Place

When Canada Place opened in 1986, it was greeted with controversy. Critics commented that its five "sails" were a poor imitation of Australia's Sydney Opera House. The complex is now a key player on the waterfront, which has grown up around it (see pp12–13).

Gastown

The cobblestone streets of Gastown have been through many reincarnations. The current one is perhaps the most satisfying. Since the 1970s, the area has worked hard to better itself. The plethora of tawdry souvenir shops have largely been replaced with boutiques selling the work of local designers, a concentration of excellent First Nations and Inuit art galleries, restaurants, and clubs. ❧ Map L3–M3

View of the sunset over Howe Sound, looking toward West Vancouver from The Lookout!

The SkyTrain, Canada Line, and SeaBus terminals are located inside Waterfront Station

Sun Tower

5 A Vancouver landmark, the 17-story Sun Tower was the tallest building in the British Commonwealth, at 270 ft (82 m), when it was built in 1911. The handsome Beaux Arts building's nine nude statues once scandalized the city, which turned out in droves in 1918 to watch Harry Gardiner, the "Human Fly," scale its walls. ◎ *100 West Pender St • Map L4*

Triangular Building, at Maple Tree Square

Chinatown

6 Stretching from Gore Avenue west to Carrall Street between Pender and Keefer streets, Chinatown dates back to the 1880s and the building of the Canadian Pacific Railway, when as many as 20,000 Chinese came to Canada. Today it is North America's second-largest Chinatown. Shops with their vegetable stalls spill onto the sidewalks. The Millennium Gate straddles Pender near Taylor Street and is the best place to start a walking tour of this lively area. ◎ *Map L4–M4*

Chinatown lamppost

Maple Tree Square

7 The city of Vancouver has its roots in this small square. Standing atop his barrel of beer, the statue of John "Gassy Jack" Deighton commemorates Gastown's founder. The talkative publican built the city's first saloon with the help of thirsty sawmill workers. A maple tree here was once a popular meeting place until it was destroyed in the Great Fire of 1886. Gaoler's Mews was the site of the city's first prison, as well as the home of the city's first policeman, Constable Jonathan Miller. ◎ *Water St at Carrall St • Map M3*

An Iron Road, Coast to Coast

The grand saga of Canadian railways is a tale of power and pain. In 1886, Prime Minister John A. Macdonald fulfilled his promise to build a cross-Canada railway to unite the new Dominion of Canada. The first transcontinental passenger train arrived in Vancouver on May 23, 1887, where Waterfront Station now stands. The whole city came out to celebrate. Even the ships in the harbor were decked out in flags. The "Iron Road" was completed at last. Sadly, progress came at the loss of many lives, including more than 600 Chinese laborers.

Vancouver Police Centennial Museum

8 Enter the old city morgue, now the police museum's forensic laboratory, and it's not difficult to imagine the coroner leaning over the slab, about to start an examination. Housed in the former Coroner Court, built in 1932, the museum has fine exhibits of counterfeit money, antique firearms, and street weaponry. Always popular is the knife room. Unsolved murders are depicted in displays complete with dummies and period costumes. ◎ *240 E Cordova St • Map M4 • 604 665 3346 • Adm*

Dr. Sun Yat-Sen Classical Chinese Garden

This Ming Dynasty-style garden, the first built outside China, opened in 1986. It re-creates the private areas typically found in a Ming scholar's home. With its meandering paths, corridors and courtyards, and asymmetrically placed rocks, the garden invites contemplation on the beauty and rhythm of nature. Plants include local and traditional Chinese varieties, such as flowering gingko trees and twisted pines. ✎ 578 Carrall St • Map M4 • 604 662 3207 • Adm

Steam Clock

Said to be the world's first steam-operated clock, this landmark is one of the most photographed in the city. But it's not an antique. Local horologist Raymond Saunders based the 16-ft- (5-m-) tall clock, at the corner of Water and Cambie streets, on an 1875 model. Be patient, and wait for the explosion of steam every 15 minutes. Erected in 1977, the bronze and gold clock strikes Westminster chimes every hour on the hour. ✎ Water St at Cambie St • Map L3

Steam clock, Gastown

A Day in Waterfront, Gastown & Chinatown

Morning

Begin at **Canada Place** (see pp12–13) for a view of the harbor. After strolling the promenade for 20 minutes, walk east to **Waterfront Station**, 601 W Cordova St, peeking at the scenic murals inside. At the junction of Cordova and Water streets, continue two blocks along Water to Cambie St to admire Gastown's **steam clock**.

Enjoy an architectural walking tour before heading to **The Irish Heather** (see p64) or **The Pourhouse** (see p65).

Afternoon

Walk east 10 minutes to **Maple Tree Square**, at Water and Carrall Sts, to see the statue of "Gassy Jack" Deighton, proprietor of the city's first saloon.

From East Cordova, head south on Carrall Street to the peaceful **Dr. Sun Yat-Sen Classical Chinese Garden**. Spend 30 minutes here, then another half hour at the adjoining **Chinese Cultural Centre Museum and Archives**.

Head east on Pender St, admiring **Millennium Gate** as you walk through it into **Chinatown**. Spend the afternoon exploring the shops, looking out for the wooden heritage buildings you pass.

End the day feasting on Cantonese dishes at **Floata Seafood** (seep 65). If the Chinatown Night Market is on (6:30pm–11pm Fri–Sun), add on a market stroll. Stay away from Vancouver's seedy side in East Hastings St, particularly at Main.

Left **The Irish Heather** Right **Chill Winston**

Bars & Clubs

The Irish Heather
There are about 100 single malts and Irish whiskeys to pick from in this attractive pub. Try the food, too – tasty pub favorites include bangers 'n' mash. ✆ 217 Carrall St • Map M4 • 604 688 9779

The Post Modern Dance Bar
State-of-the-art sound and light systems keep this ultra-modern dance club buzzing. ✆ 7 Alexander St • Map M4 • 604 647 0121

The Blarney Stone
Friday and Saturday nights guarantee a rip-roaring, feet-stomping crowd at this legendary Irish pub and nightclub. ✆ 216 Carrall St • Map M4 • 604 687 4322

Cascades Lounge
Sip a refreshing cocktail and nibble seafood snacks, such as porcini-dusted scallops, while enjoying spectacular views of the North Shore and Stanley Park. Live jazz on weekends. Patio in summer. ✆ Pan Pacific Hotel, 300-999 Canada Place Way • Map L2 • 604 895 2480

Steamworks Brewing
Complement your pizza, pasta, burger, or satay with one of the several delicious beers brewed here, such as pale ale, nutbrown, or stout. ✆ 375 Water St • Map L3 • 604 689 2739

The Cambie
Pouring drinks since 1887, The Cambie serves mainly thirsty 20-somethings these days. Cheap micro-brews are the big draw. ✆ 300 Cambie St • Map M4 • 604 684 6466

Shine NightClub
Dance to DJ-driven music, including rock, rap, electro, dance hall, and reggae. The club has two rooms: one blasts electro/hip hop/rock and the other features tamer dance music. ✆ 364 Water St • Map L3 • 604 408 4321

Alibi Room
DJs play funk, soul, and hip-hop in this warm two-level space. Catch art shows and movie screenings in the lower lounge. A great place to meet people. Craft beers on tap. ✆ 157 Alexander St • Map M3 • 604 623 3383

Chill Winston
Situated in the heart of Gastown, Chill Winston is a hip, young bar with a cool vibe. The huge patio is great for people-watching in summer. ✆ 3 Alexander St • Map M3 • 604 288 9575

Lobby Lounge
See and be seen at the Fairmont Pacific Rim's stylish lounge bar, which features daily live music by popular local artists. ✆ 1038 Canada Place • Map L3 • 604 695 5300

Note: Unless otherwise stated, all bars, clubs, and restaurants accept credit cards

Price Categories

For a three-course meal for one with half a bottle of wine (or equivalent meal), taxes, and extra charges.

$	under $20
$$	$20–$35
$$$	$35–$60
$$$$	$60–$85
$$$$$	over $85

Above **The Pourhouse Bar**

🔟 Restaurants & Cafés

1 Chambar
Moules-frites are a specialty at this hugely popular Belgian restaurant, where the cocktail menu makes a great way to start the evening. 🔷 *562 Beatty St • Map L4 • 604 879 7119 • $$$$$*

2 Wildebeest
Critics are raving about this eatery with cocktails that complement the menu and eclectic, innovative dishes focused on whole-animal cookery, such as pork jowl and beef tongue. 🔷 *120 West Hastings St • Map L3 • 604 687 6880 • $$$$*

3 L'Abattoir
L'Abattoir offers fine dining in an informal setting of refurbished brick and beam. The menu features French-influenced West Coast fare at its best. 🔷 *217 Carrall St • Map M4 • 604 568 1701 • $$$$$*

4 Salt Tasting Room
Tucked away in historic Blood Alley, Salt specializes in artisan cheeses, small-batch cured meats, and a dynamic array of wines, sherries, and ports. 🔷 *45 Blood Alley • Map L3 • 604 633 1912 • $$$*

5 Momo Sushi
Fresh sushi is the draw here, with teriyaki, tempura, and sashimi also available. Expect line-ups at lunch. 🔷 *6-375 Water St • Map L3 • 604 683 7632 • $$*

6 Wild Rice
Upbeat house music beckons you to try spicy, modern Chinese cuisine in this cozy space. Small but good wine list. 🔷 *117 W Pender St • Map L4 • 604 642 2882 • $$*

7 Al Porto Ristorante
Pastas, fish, meat, and pizza are the highlights at this bright, lively Italian *trattoria*. More than 200 wines on offer, 80 from BC. 🔷 *321 Water St • Map L3 • 604 683 8376 • $$$*

8 The Pourhouse
The inexpensive and interesting pub food served here includes espresso-braised short ribs and a po'boy sandwich lunch special. There is plenty of room for drinkers at the long bar. 🔷 *162 Water St • Map L3 • 604 568 7022 • $$$*

9 Brioche Urban Baking
Diners cram into this 30-seat café, enjoying the casually trendy ambience and the rustic Italian meals and baked goods. Take out available. 🔷 *401 W Cordova St • Map L3 • 604 682 4037 • $*

🔟 Floata Seafood Restaurant
Delectable *dim sum* dishes arrive in a flurry of carts. There's also a Cantonese-style menu. 🔷 *180 Keefer St • Map M4 • 604 602 0368 • $$$*

Following pages Downtown Vancouver by night

Left **Shoppers, Robson Street** Right **Cyclists, False Creek Seawalk**

Downtown

VANCOUVER'S DOWNTOWN CORE *is a blend of old and new, all nicely contained in a walkable package that extends from BC Place Stadium to the West End. The city's first church sits at the corner of Georgia and Burrard streets, hemmed in by glass-walled office towers. The landmark Fairmont Hotel Vancouver graces the opposite corner, a glorious reminder of yesteryear. Alive with activity, downtown hums all day and much of the night. The core includes high-density residential areas, street and mall shopping, theaters, music venues, restaurants, and nightclubs, all adding up to a pleasant, invigorating energy.*

TOP 10 Sights

1. Robson Street
2. Christ Church Cathedral
3. Fairmont Hotel Vancouver
4. Library Square
5. Vancouver Art Gallery
6. Pacific Centre
7. BC Sports Hall of Fame & Museum
8. Science World
9. False Creek Seawalk
10. Robson Square and Law Courts

Stained glass, Christ Church Cathedral

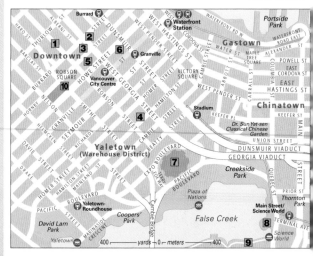

Robson Street

1 West End residents, the city's urban chic, international celebrities, and tourists alike flock to Robson Street to join the bustle of shoppers. Part of the fun is people watching over a specialty coffee, then browsing the brand name and independent Canadian and international shops. Slip down a side street to get a taste of the historic West End, Canada's most densely populated area. ◈ *Map H2–K4*

Christ Church Cathedral

2 A gem in the heart of the city and once a beacon for mariners entering Vancouver's harbor, Christ Church Cathedral, consecrated in 1895, was designed in the Gothic Revival style. The interior has impressive old-growth Douglas fir ceiling beams. Three of the 32 stained-glass windows are by the British artist William Morris; look for them in the office vestibule. As part of a major renovation, a Kenneth Jones organ was installed. ◈ *690 Burrard St • Map K3 • 604 682 3848*

Fairmont Hotel Vancouver

Fairmont Hotel Vancouver

3 Begun in 1928 by the Canadian Pacific Railway, construction on the city's most famous hotel halted with the 1929 stock market crash. Its steel skeleton sat until 1939, when it was hastily finished for the visit of King George VI. Features include a steep copper roof with impish gargoyles. Stroll through the lobby and enjoy afternoon tea or a drink in the lounge, while admiring the lavishness. ◈ *900 W Georgia St • Map K3 • 604 684 3131*

Library Square

4 The Vancouver Central Library, designed in part by renowned architect Moshe Safdie, opened in 1995. At first critized by some for its resemblance to a Roman coliseum, it soon became universally popular. Library Square takes up a whole city block, and includes the library; a seven-story, glass-roofed promenade; the Federal Tower, housing government offices; souvenir shops, a coffee bar, and take-out restaurants. The promenade is an ideal place to relax and people watch. ◈ *Corner of Robson & Homer sts • Map K4*

Vancouver Public Library, Library Square

Fountains at the Vancouver Art Gallery

5 Vancouver Art Gallery
When the Court House was erected in 1912, designed by Francis Rattenbury, one of BC's flashiest architects, its solid form symbolized the British Empire at its peak. Another controversial architect, Arthur Erickson, supervised the redesign of the building when it became the Vancouver Art Gallery in the mid-1980s. Inside, the Emily Carr collection is Canada's largest. Contemporary photoconceptual work also has a prominent place (see pp18–19).

6 Pacific Centre
Quality department stores including The Bay anchor the host of smaller shops in this huge

mall, which features cascading fountains and a three-story waterfall. Restaurants and take-aways dot the concourse.
⬥ 609 Granville St with entrances via Robson, Dunsmuir & W Georgia sts • Map K3 • 604 688 7235 • Open 10am–7pm Mon, Tue & Sat, 10am–9pm Wed–Fri, 11am–6pm Sun

7 BC Sports Hall of Fame and Museum
Twenty galleries showcase BC's sports history from the 1860s onward in a 20,000 sq ft (1,858 sq m) space located in BC Place Stadium (see p42). Interactive displays provide fascinating details of the lives of famous athletes such as skier Nancy Green and sprinter Harry Jerome. The Participation Gallery is especially fun for kids. ⬥ 777 Pacific Blvd S, Gate A • Map L4 • 604 687 5520 • Adm

8 Science World
The striking geodesic dome housing Science World's many interactive galleries and travelling exhibitions was built for Expo '86. Visitors can play with magnetic liquids, touch animal skin and bones, and check out exhibits on motion, and energy, as well as laser shows. The OMNIMAX® Theatre's giant screen fits into the dome's curves (see pp22–3).

Terry Fox's Marathon of Hope

Born in Winnipeg in 1958, Terry Fox grew up in a Vancouver suburb. When just 18 years old, he was diagnosed with bone cancer and had his leg amputated. Three years later, in 1980, Terry dipped his artificial leg into the Atlantic Ocean, beginning his Marathon of Hope across Canada to raise money for cancer research. After 143 days and 3,339 miles (5,373 km), Terry stopped his run. Cancer had spread to his lungs. He died in 1981, shortly after realizing his dream of raising $1 for every Canadian – over $24 million. Annual Terry Fox runs worldwide continue Terry's mission.

Interactive display, Science World

9 False Creek Seawalk

False Creek (see p79) once covered an extensive part of the downtown area. It now ends at Quebec Street, site of Science World. The paved False Creek Seawalk joins English Bay Seawalk just east of Burrard Bridge and circles the creek. It's ideal for in-line skaters, cyclists, and walkers. Access to False Creek ferries is available at several points along the seawalk. ◈ Map H6–M5

Plexiglass dome, Robson Square

10 Robson Square and Law Courts

Spanning several blocks, the four-level Robson Square was designed by BC architect Arthur Erickson. On the south side of Robson Street, a cascading waterfall and trees cool the steps near Spring, a red steel sculpture by Alan Chung Hung. On the level above, inside the Law Courts, is a pond with seating and a good view. Jack Harman's sculpture, Themis Goddess of Justice, presides over the Great Hall, with its expanses of glass. ◈ 800 block Robson St • Map J4 • 604 660 8989

A Downtown Walk

Morning

🕐 Start at **BC Place Stadium** (see p42), exploring the **BC Sports Hall of Fame and Museum** for about an hour. Exiting the museum, head west toward Robson St, passing by the **Terry Fox Memorial**, a tribute to the local hero who raised millions of dollars for cancer research.

Continue west three blocks along Robson St to Homer St, and **Library Square** (see p69). Drop in to have a look at the building's airy promenade before walking west on Robson St to **Pacific Centre**. Peruse the shops for about an hour, then exit the mall and cross Howe St to the **Vancouver Art Gallery**. Enjoy a salad and sandwich in its casually elegant **Gallery Café**, snagging a patio table if weather permits.

Afternoon

After lunch, head to the fourth floor of the **Vancouver Art Gallery** (see pp18–19) and the wonderful **Emily Carr Collection**. Begin by watching the 15-minute video about this remarkable painter of forests and totem poles.

Exiting the gallery, cross Robson St and stroll through lovely **Robson Square**. Then it's on to shopping along **Robson Street** (see p69). Satisfy a sweet tooth at one of the several chocolate shops. Loop back to Burrard St.

End the day with a treat at **Kamei Royale Japanese Restaurant** (see p73), at 1030 W Georgia St. The excellent sushi chefs welcome you enthusiastically.

Left **lululemon atheltica** Right **Daniel Le Chocolat Belge**

🔟 Shopping

Roots Canada
Classic Canadian-designed sportswear and leatherwear, including a wide range of accessories, from watches to belts and backpacks. ✆ *1001 Robson St • Map J3 • 604 683 4305*

lululemon athletica
This Vancouver-based company sells wildly popular men's and women's yoga apparel, athletic gear, and casual wear. ✆ *1148 Robson St • Map J3 • 604 681 3118*

Bute Street Liquor Store
This large BC Liquor Store carries an extensive variety of well-displayed wines, spirits, beers, and BC ice wine, made from frozen grapes. ✆ *1155 Bute St • Map J3 • 604 660 4569*

Rendezvous Art Gallery
Contemporary and traditional Canadian paintings and sculptures reflect West Coast beauty. First Nations and Inuit artists are well represented. ✆ *323 Howe St • Map K3 • 604 687 7466*

Daniel Le Chocolat Belge
Belgian chocolate and all-natural or organic ingredients are used to create the delicious pralines and champagne, coffee, and lemon truffles sold here. ✆ *1105 Robson St • Map J3 • 604 688 9624*

Holt Renfrew
This uniquely Canadian brand dates back to the early 1800s. The iconic Vancouver store offers instore boutiques, including Loui Vuitton and Chanel, plus its own relatively affordable line. ✆ *737 Dunsmuir St • Map K3 • 604 681 3121*

Aritzia
The haunt of trendy Vancouverites, Aritzia is a homegrown store selling cool clothing. ✆ *1110 Robson St • Map K4 • 604 684 3251*

John Fluevog Boots & Shoes Ltd
Fluevog's funky and trendy, yet sturdy, shoes and boots are snapped up by the fashion savvy. ✆ *837 Granville St • Map K4 • 604 688 282*

Tiffany & Co
Here's your chance to buy something in the legendary blue box from the famous New York jewelry store. ✆ *723 Burrard St • Map J3 • 604 630 1300*

Murchie's Tea & Coffee
The Murchie family began selecting, blending, and selling fairtrade tea and coffee in 1894 and the tradition continues today ✆ *825 West Pender St • Map K3 • 604 669 0783*

Price Categories

For a three-course meal for one with half a bottle of wine (or equivalent meal), taxes, and extra charges.

$	under $20
$$	$20–$35
$$$	$35–$60
$$$$	$60–$85
$$$$$	over $85

Above **Coast**

Restaurants

1 Kamei Royale Japanese Restaurant

Delight in traditional grilled dishes, or in the house-original rolls at the sushi bar. ✎ *1030 W Georgia St • Map K3 • 604 687 8588 • $$$*

2 Forage

The latest gathering spot for locavores is all about sustainable dining. Forage's innovative cuisine showcases dishes made with local and organic produce. ✎ *1300 Robson St • Map K4 • 604 661 1400 • $$$*

3 Cibo Trattoria

Located in the trendy Moda Hotel, Cibo serves authentic Italian cuisine made with fresh organic ingredients. ✎ *Moda Hotel, 900 Seymour St • Map K4 • 604 602 9570 • $$$$*

4 CinCin Ristorante & Bar

Delicious rotisserie meats, pasta, and risotto are served in this large Italian-themed restaurant popular with visiting Hollywood stars. ✎ *1154 Robson St • Map J3 • 604 688 7338 • $$$$*

5 Diva at the Met

In the open kitchen, chefs conjure up gastronomical magic. The exceptional wine list is topped with BC wines. ✎ *Metropolitan Hotel, 645 Howe St • Map K3 • 604 602 7788 • $$$$*

6 Salathai Thai Restaurant

Enjoy tasty Thai food prepared with home-made sauces, served in a tropical setting. Friendly, attentive service. ✎ *102-888 Burrard St • Map J3 • 604 683 7999 • $$*

7 Coast

This vibrant two-storey room showcases BC's finest, freshest fish and seafood – try one of the seafood towers. ✎ *1054 Alberni St • Map J3 • 604 685 5010 • $$$$*

8 Raincity Grill

Pacific waters lap outside this trend-setting English Bay restaurant; sunsets are a bonus. The focus is on regional, seasonal, and organic food. ✎ *1193 Denman St • Map G3 • 604 685 7337 • $$$$*

9 Le Crocodile

Alsatian tart has been the signature dish at this elegant French restaurant for many years. Its selection of French wines is a highlight. ✎ *100-909 Burrard St • Map J3 • 604 669 4298 • $$$$*

10 Hawksworth

Delicious contemporary cuisine is the order of the day at this restaurant in the legendary Hotel Georgia. ✎ *801 W Georgia St • Map K3 • 604 673 7000 • $$$$$*

Left **Railway Club** Right **The Roxy**

Bars and Clubs

Ceili's Irish Pub
About as Irish as you'll get in Vancouver, the aptly named Ceili's (meaning "gathering of friends for food, drink, and good times") is packed every night. Live music adds to the night time buzz from Wednesday through to Saturday. ✆ 670 Smithe St • Map J4 • 604 697 9199

Commodore Ballroom
A Vancouver institution since 1929, the club hosts ticketed rock, pop, blues, and jazz acts. ✆ 868 Granville St • Map K4 • 604 739 4550 • www.livenation.com

Barcelona Ultra Lounge
A popular club that styles itself after the boutique clubs of Miami, New York, and London with its glitzy decor and state-of-the-art sound system. ✆ 1180 Granville St • Map J4 • 604 249 5151

Caprice Nightclub
Upscale club with two levels and a huge dance floor. Top 40 and retro nights. ✆ 967 Granville St • Map K4 • 604 685 3288

Railway Club
Live country, folk, roots, and funk at this legendary club. Microbrews, quality wines, and scotch and martini lists. ✆ 579 Dunsmuir St • Map K3 • 604 681 1625

ginger 62
Live and spun house, reggae, R&B, and soul at this retro-style lounge. Tasty snacks forestall the effects of specialty martinis and cocktails. ✆ 1219 Granville St • Map J4 • 604 688 5494

Venue
The home of Vancouver's alternative music scene, Venue has live bands and a wrap-around balcony with terrific views. ✆ 881 Granville St • Map K4 • 604 646 0064

AuBAR Nightclub
Top 40 selections reverberate off the lofty ceiling while candlelit tables inspire romantic whisperings. Dress to impress. ✆ 674 Seymour St • Map K3 • 604 648 2227

Yew Bar
The bartenders become performance artists at this chic bar in the Four Seasons Hotel. Food is served on a communal dining table. ✆ 791 W Georgia St • Map K3 • 604 689 9333

The Roxy
Where the locals go to dance to local and Canadian bands. Hugely popular during the weekends, so arrive early. ✆ 932 Granville St • Map K4 • 604 331 7999

Call ahead to check opening hours, as times may vary according to the day of the week. Some nightclubs are closed Sundays

Price Categories

For a three-course meal for one with half a bottle of wine (or equivalent meal), taxes, and extra charges.

$	under $20
$$	$20–$35
$$$	$35–$60
$$$$	$60–$85
$$$$$	over $85

Above **The Gallery Café**

Cheap Eats

1 Fish Shack
With seafood as fresh as the crowd that dines there, this casual eatery is fun and inexpensive – time it right for "buck a shuck" oysters. ☜ *1026 Granville St • Map J4 • 604 678 1049 • $$*

2 Kintaro
Expect lots of slurping at the counter of this no-frills *ramenya*, which is wildly popular for its BBQ pork *shio*. ☜ *788 Denman St • Map H2 • 604 682 7568 • $*

3 Library Square
Find a table and energize with a slice of Flying Wedge pizza, or choose between a Blenz coffee with a Rocky Road square and a Yogen Früz yogurt cone. ☜ *345 Robson St • Map K4 • $*

4 Fujiya
Made to order take-out sushi and the freshest sashimi, served either in individual bento boxes or on sushi trays for large groups. ☜ *12-1060 Pender St • Map K3 • 604 608 1050 • $$*

5 Bellaggio Café
Snag a booth in this stylish Italian restaurant, and be sure to ask about the daily pasta special, served with garlic bread. BC wines featured. ☜ *773 Hornby St • Map K3 • 604 408 1281 • $*

6 Pacific Centre Food Fair
Choose from Japanese or Chinese made-to-order dishes, pizza, burgers, tacos, juices, and frozen yogurts. ☜ *Granville & Dunsmuir sts entrance • Map K3 • 604 688 7235 • $*

7 The Gallery Café
Choose from a range of soups, salads, and sandwiches, then peruse the exhibitions at the Vancouver Art Gallery *(see pp18–19)*. ☜ *750 Hornby St • Map K3 • 604 688 2233 • $*

8 Pita Wrap Cafe
Middle Eastern-style meat or vegetarian combos and falafel wraps at this tiny takeout require two hands to hold. ☜ *565 Dunsmuir St • Map K3 • 604 681 7634 • $*

9 Urban Fare
The gourmet grocery store's restaurant serves up salads, soups, and a buffet made with the freshest ingredients. ☜ *1133 Alberni St • Map J3 • 604 669 5831 • $$*

10 La Vieille France
Crepes are the specialty at this utilitarian spot. The berry and cream cheese, and spinach and feta are favorites. ☜ *380 Robson St • Map K4 • 604 689 9885 • $*

Gourmet Food Carts are found on busy downtown street corners. Look for Re-Up BBQ and Fresh Local Wild

Left *Gate to the Pacific Northwest,* Vanier Park Right **Boy mummy, Museum of Vancouver**

South Granville & Yaletown

THE NEIGHBORHOODS OF SOUTH GRANVILLE AND YALETOWN *are sepa-rated by a drive across Granville Bridge or a ferry ride across False Creek. On the south shore, South Granville offers a pleasant mix of upscale shops and restaurants. Granville Island is a bustling labyrinth of converted warehouses overlooking False Creek. The centerpiece is the large public market. Yaletown, on the north shore of the creek, began life as a railway works yard. Since the early 1990s, Yaletown has undergone a furiously fast transformation. The once-decrepit area now booms with offices, condos, boutiques, nightclubs, brew pubs, and restaurants.*

🔟 Sights

1. Granville Island
2. Sunset Beach
3. Vancouver Maritime Museum
4. Gallery Row
5. Roundhouse Arts & Recreation Centre
6. H.R. MacMillan Space Centre
7. Vanier Park
8. Yaletown Warehouse District
9. False Creek
10. Museum of Vancouver

RCMP schooner, Vancouver Maritime Museum

A slew of commercial art galleries have earned South Granville Street between 5th and 15th avenues the nickname Gallery Row

View of West End high-rises from Granville Island

1 Granville Island

The original mud flats of False Creek were a fishing ground for the Squamish people. Industry moved in, polluting much of the turn-of-the-19th-century city. In the 1970s, all that changed with the redevelopment of Granville Island. Under the aegis of the federal government, heavy industry moved out and Granville Island quickly became a colorful, bustling community. Free street parking is available with a three-hour limit, or choose paid parking in covered lots (see pp20–21).

2 Sunset Beach

The white sands of Sunset Beach, which marks the end of the English Bay seawall and the start of False Creek, provide an ideal setting for relaxing, tanning, or swimming. Summertime water temperatures rise to 65°F (18°C), and lifeguards are on duty from mid-May to Labour Day. The western end of Sunset Beach provides a good view of the gray granite Inukshuk (see p36). The Vancouver Aquatic Centre, at the east end of the beach, has an Olympic-size swimming and diving pools, a sauna, a whirlpool, and a steam room. False Creek Ferries (see p21) dock behind the center. ◈ Map G3–H4

3 Vancouver Maritime Museum

Highlights of the West Coast's rich maritime history include sea-going canoes and a 1928 RCMP schooner. Kids can play with the discovery center's telescopes, computer games, and underwater robot (see p34). ◈ 1905 Ogden Ave • Map G4 • 604 257 8300 • Open Sep–May: 10am–5pm Tue–Sat, noon–5pm Sun; May–Sep: 10am–5pm daily • Adm

4 Gallery Row

Sixteen art and antique galleries line the four-block stretch of Granville Street between 5th Avenue and West Broadway. There is no greater concentration of galleries in the city. ◈ 2100-2400 Granville St • Map H6

View of Sunset Beach

5 Roundhouse Arts & Recreation Centre

Located on Beach Avenue in a former Canadian Pacific Railway switching building, the Roundhouse includes theater and gallery spaces and a host of community arts and athletic programs. It also houses the locomotive that pulled the first passenger train to Vancouver in 1887 in a splendid glassed-in space.
⌖ 181 Roundhouse Mews
• Map K5 • 604 713 1800

Plaque, Roundhouse

6 H.R. MacMillan Space Centre

Space lore is presented in child-friendly, hands-on displays and multimedia shows at the space center. A demonstration theater, the Virtual Voyages' full-motion simulator, and the Cosmic Courtyard's interactive gallery bring space to life. The Planetarium's multimedia shows feature space and astronomy inside a 65-ft (20-m) dome, and its laser shows set to music are always popular. ⌖ 1100 Chestnut St
• Map G4 • 604 738 7827 • Adm

Yaletown's Railway History

Yaletown was first settled by Canadian Pacific Railway (CPR) train crews and laborers who arrived after the CPR closed its construction camp in Yale, BC, on completion of the transcontinental railway to Vancouver in 1887. In the early 1990s, Yaletown was still the decaying heart of the city's remaining industrial activity, when a development plan jump-started its transformation into a lively urban area. In just over a decade, Yaletown has become Vancouver's hottest community.

---

7 Vanier Park

Vanier Park is a calming oasis in the midst of the city. Boats sail by on English Bay, kites fly overhead, and pedestrians and cyclists pass through on their way to Kitsilano Beach or Granville Island. Coast Salish people once inhabited the park area. It is now home to the H.R. MacMillan Space Centre, Museum of Vancouver, and Vancouver Maritime Museum (see p77). ⌖ Map G4

8 Yaletown Warehouse District

Warehouses have been transformed into lofts and stores, café terraces have sprung up on old loading docks, and high-rises have filled Yaletown's skyline. Along with the new residents has come a facelift. Homer, Hamilton, and Mainland streets have been spruced up, making the most of heritage architectural features, including red brick and arched doorways. Numerous brew pubs and nightclubs keep the area hopping at night. ⌖ Map J4–K5

Renovated warehouses, Yaletown

Boats moored on False Creek, south side

9 False Creek

As its name implies, False Creek is not a creek at all but a saltwater inlet. In the heart of the city, it extends east from Burrard Bridge to Science World *(see pp22–3)*. In the 1850s, Captain G.H. Richards sailed up this body of water, which then covered what is now Chinatown, eastward to Clark Drive, hoping to find the Fraser River. Disappointed, he named it False Creek. The mud flats Richards saw served as fishing grounds for the Squamish people. Sawmills later set up on the south shore, railyards on the north. Today, paved paths flank both sides *(see p71)*, and boats and small ferries *(see p21)* ply the waters. ◈ Map J6–L5

10 Museum of Vancouver

Canada's largest civic museum boasts re-creations of Vancouver's history, from a fur-trading post to an amazing display of neon signs. Artifacts from a huge collection, much of it donated by locals, make up natural history, archaeology, Asian arts, and ethnology exhibits. The Egyptian boy mummy is one of the biggest attractions. ◈ 1100 Chestnut St • Map G5 • 604 736 4431 • Open 10am–5pm Tue–Sun, Thu to 9pm • Adm

A Day in Yaletown & at Granville Island

Morning

🕐 Start in **Yaletown** at the corner of Drake and Hamilton streets for a 15-minute stroll north on Hamilton, noting its historic buildings. At Helmcken St, turn right, then right again at Mainland St. Spend half an hour in the shops, ending at **The Cross Decor & Design** *(see p81)*.

Cross Pacific Blvd to admire the **Roundhouse's** Steam Train 374. Take 15 minutes exploring the complex, then hop on the **Aquabus** *(see p21)* from the dock behind the center for the short trip to Granville Island *(see pp20–21)*. For a fun hour, wander the public market, buying food for a casual lunch on a waterside bench.

Afternoon

Exit the market's east side. Continue on Johnston St past **Ocean Concrete**. Turn right on Old Bridge St to watch the glass blower at **New-Small and Sterling Glass Studio** *(see p20)*. Walk to **Railspur District**, on your left. Browse the shops for 20 minutes, then cross adjacent Railspur Park to Cartwright St. Turn left and walk to the end, to **Ron Basford Park**, where kids love running up and down "the mound."

Back on Johnston St, head west to peek at the modern art in the **Charles H. Scott Gallery** *(see p35)*. Head towards Vanier Park to find the **Museum of Vancouver** *(see left)*, allowing yourself an hour there.

🍴 End the day at **The Sandbar** (1535 Johnston St) for views of the market, False Creek, and the West End.

For a pleasant under-one-hour trip round False Creek, catch a mini-ferry from one of the Granville Island docks **See pp20–21**

79

Left **Fresh striped pasta, specialty food stall** Right **Hat display, craft stall**

Granville Island Public Market

1 Public Market Building
At Granville Island's west end is the large public market, housed in part in a wood-frame, corrugated tin-clad warehouse. Built in the early 1920s by the Island's first tenant, BC Equipment, this structure set the architectural style of the Island. The timbered beams and massive pulleys and hooks once pulled rope coils from one area to the other. *See pp20–21.*

2 Food Courts
Two food courts offer sit-down and takeaway food, including Greek, Mexican, Thai, Chinese, and Canadian. Patience and strategy may be required to land one of the limited indoor tables.

3 Local Produce and Seafood
Artful displays tempt with fruits and vegetables – much of it organic – fresh from the orchards and farms of BC. Okanagan cherries, apples, and peaches are a summer delight. BC wild salmon is another market specialty – both fresh and smoked in gift boxes.

4 Olde World Fudge
Irresistible Belgian chocolate treats are concocted on-site in a copper vat. Assorted gift boxes include fudge, toffee, brittles, and caramel apples. Samples available!

5 Stuart's Bakery
Mouth-watering pies, chocolate confections, and pastries fill one counter; multigrain, cheese, and other loaves crowd the other.

6 Eating Outdoors
Enjoy your takeaway food or just relax at the rustic seating areas overlooking False Creek. Exit the west side of the market for views of the marina. On the east side, enjoy free entertainment in the Market Courtyard. The courtyard's worn floor planks from its days as an industrial dock add to the charm.

7 Craft and Specialty Stalls
Day vendors sell an assortment of locally made wares, including seasonal and specialty items. Bowls made of BC wood, Thai curry sauces, herb seedlings, homemade pies, and jewelry are just the start. Vendors may not be located in the same place from day to day.

8 Buskers
Licensed musicians, magicians, clowns, jugglers, and other talented folk entertain free of charge, though a donation is always appreciated.

9 Flower Shops
Abundance and quality are the themes at the market's flower shops. It is worth a stop just to admire the gorgeous blooms and take in the heady scents.

10 Marina
At the marina on the market's west side you'll find fancy yachts, simple sail boats, and the occasional fishing boat. Tall ships dock here during festivals.

Left **Hand-blown glass cups, Circle Craft Co-op** Right **The latest fashions, Boboli**

Shopping

Meinhardts
This iconic south Granville food emporium has a similar design to NYC's famous Dean & DeLuca and is based around the concept of buying fresh ingredients on a regular basis. ✆ *3002 Granville St • Map B2 • 604 732 4405*

The Cross Decor & Design
Located in a 1914 heritage building, this fabulous store sources items from all over the world, and also features pieces by local artists and vendors. ✆ *1198 Homer St • Map J5 • 604 689 2900*

Bernstein & Gold
Carry or ship home Egyptian cotton linens, Italian bedding, tapestries, and leather journals, Fornasetti plates, cashmere throws, and Fortuni lamps. ✆ *1168 Hamilton St • Map K5 • 604 687 1535*

Swirl Wine Store
This shop sells the best selection of BC wines at vineyard prices, as well as gourmet gift baskets. ✆ *1185 Mainland St • Map K5 • 604 408 9463*

Circle Craft Co-op
The best of BC crafts, from handmade clothing to one-of-a-kind jewelry to wall art, ceramics, and hand-blown glass. ✆ *1666 Johnston St • Map H5 • 604 669 8021*

Freedman Shoes
Since 1931 Freedman has brought its customers the best in stylish footwear and is a Granville landmark. Featured brands include Converse, Dr. Martens, Ted Baker and Timberland. ✆ *2867 Granville St • Map B2 • 604 732 5011*

Forge and Form
High-end gold and silver jewelry with precious stones. Bold rings, fluid necklaces. ✆ *1334 Cartwright St • Map H5 • 604 684 6298*

Basquiat
This stylish, friendly clothing boutique sells exclusive European labels and American seasonal lines for men and women. ✆ *1189 Hamilton St • Map J5 • 604 688 0828*

Malaspina Printmakers Gallery
Prints by Canadian (particularly BC) and international artists with images and styles – from photo-realism to abstract – to suit all tastes. ✆ *1555 Duranleau St • Map H5 • 604 688 1724*

Boboli
Trend-setting styles from a variety of men's and women's lines, including Missoni, Etro, and Blumarine. Free alterations. ✆ *2776 Granville St • Map B2 • 604 257 2300*

Head south of the Granville Bridge for stores, boutiques, and restaurants, as well as a beautifully restored theater

Left **George Ultra Lounge** Right **The New Oxford**

🔟 Clubs & Bars

1 Venue
This live music destination boasts a huge split-level room that can hold 500 people and plays host to some of the city's top alternative DJs. 🟊 *881 Granville St • Map K4 • 604 646 0064*

2 Vancouver FanClub
Strut your stuff on an elevated catwalk or boogie on the mezzanine dance floor at this eclectic dancing and dining venue. 🟊 *1050 Granville St • Map J4 • 604 689 7720*

3 Yaletown Brewing Company
Enjoy locally brewed beer here while dining on homestyle cooking in the pub, the restaurant, or on the popular patio. 🟊 *1111 Mainland St • Map K5 • 604 681 2739*

4 The New Oxford
A 50-ft (15-m) long bar is the centerpiece at this tongue-in-cheek nod to Oxford University and British sporting culture. 🟊 *1144 Homer St • Map J4 • 604 899 3229*

5 Bar None
In a converted warehouse, this New York style nightclub draws a hip urban crowd. Live music, a spacious dance floor, and ample seating. 🟊 *1222 Hamilton St • Map J5 • 604 689 7000*

6 The Refinery
This new world eatery and cocktail bar with an old world atmosphere attracts sustainability-conscious diners and experienced cocktailers alike. 🟊 *1115 Granville St • Map J4 • 604 687 8001*

7 Dockside Restaurant and Brewing Company
Savor the delicious beer brewed here while admiring the boats on False Creek. Great patio. 🟊 *Granville Island Hotel, 1253 Johnston St • Map H6 • 604 685 7070*

8 Backstage Lounge
This low-key hangout attracts theatergoers and actors from the Granville Island Stage next door. Live music and jams, with a focus on local talent. 🟊 *1585 Johnston St • Map H5 • 604 687 1354*

9 George Ultra Lounge
This trendy spot for the well-heeled cocktail crowd features London-influenced modern mixology in a gorgeous room with velvet banquettes. 🟊 *1137 Hamilton St • Map K4 • 604 628 5555*

10 Opus Bar
This sophisticated hotel bar attracts a glamorous crowd. Caribbean-inspired cocktails are delicious but pricey. 🟊 *350 Davie St • Map K5 • 604 642 6787*

Price Categories

For a three-course meal for one with half a bottle of wine (or equivalent meal), taxes and extra charges.

$	under $20
$$	$20–$35
$$$	$35–$60
$$$$	$60–$85
$$$$$	over $85

Above **Waterside patio, The Sandbar**

Restaurants

Blue Water Café and Raw Bar
Inventive West Coast dishes made with the freshest local fish, and sushi made with coastal shellfish, are masterfully prepared here. Excellent wine list. ◈ *1095 Hamilton St • Map K4 • 604 688 8078 • $$$$*

C Restaurant
Dishes such as blueberry salmon gravlax make for loyal customers at this restaurant taking a stand on sustainability. ◈ *1600 Howe St • Map H5 • 604 681 1164 • $$$$$*

West
Vancouver's perennial favorite serves contemporary regional cuisine and houses a highly-awarded wine collection. ◈ *2881 Granville St • Map B2 • 604 738 8938 • $$$$$*

Cioppino's Mediterranean Grill
Chef "Pino" Posteraro creates delicious lighter versions of traditional Italian pasta, risottos, and seafood dishes. ◈ *1133 Hamilton St • Map J5 • 604 688 7466 • $$$$*

Provence Marinaside
This restaurant and bar is one of the prettiest places on False Creek. A sommelier is on hand to help select the wine. Picnic baskets available. ◈ *1177 Marinaside Cres • Map K5 • 604 681 4144 • $$$$*

glowbal grill & satay bar
This celeb-spotting hotspot is renowned for its tapas, steaks, and of course satays. Superb wine list. ◈ *1079 Mainland St • Map K4 • 604 602 0835 • $$$$*

Rodney's Oyster House
The action is at the counter, so sidle up and order any of 12 to 20 oyster varieties, shucked as you watch. Steamed clams and mussels, crab, and Atlantic lobster are also featured. ◈ *1228 Hamilton St • Map J5 • 604 609 0080 • $$$$*

Brix
Diners head to Brix for game and fresh fish favorites, including Yukon Arctic char, and to enjoy the romantic courtyard. ◈ *1138 Homer St • Map J5 • 604 915 9463 • $$$*

Edible Canada
A must-have at this bistro is the salmon cooked to perfection paired with the Blue Mountain pinot noir. ◈ *1596 Johnston St • Map H6 • 604 682 6681 • $$$$*

The Sandbar
Feast on Dungeness crab cakes and cedar-planked salmon while enjoying breathtaking views of False Creek, English Bay, and the West End. ◈ *1535 Johnston St • Map H5 • 604 669 9030 • $$$$*

Left **Main Library, University of British Columbia** Right **BC Ferry, Horseshoe Bay**

Greater Vancouver & Beyond

ONE OF THE REASONS *Vancouver is so often listed among the top ten cities of the world in which to live is the wide range of things to do, and the breathtakingly lovely scenery in which to do them, just a short drive away from the downtown core. Sandy beaches, rugged coastlines, and popular ski hills are minutes away. The ski slopes and golf courses of Whistler are reached after a scenic two-hour drive, ideal for an overnight excursion. Splendid rainforests can be enjoyed in the University of British Columbia's Pacific Spirit Regional Park and in North Vancouver's Capilano Suspension Bridge Park. Towns such as Squamish or Brackendale provide unforgettable nature walks, hikes and climbs, affording glimpses of the region's flora and fauna. Some small waterfront towns such as Steveston, a former fishing village, have proudly preserved their local history.*

Totem pole,
Capilano Park

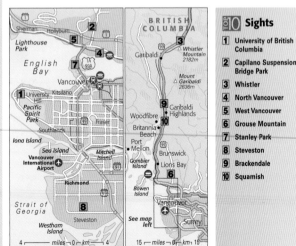

🔟 Sights

1. **University of British Columbia**
2. **Capilano Suspension Bridge Park**
3. **Whistler**
4. **North Vancouver**
5. **West Vancouver**
6. **Grouse Mountain**
7. **Stanley Park**
8. **Steveston**
9. **Brackendale**
10. **Squamish**

Avoid getting caught in central Vancouver rush hour traffic when making excursions to destinations beyond the city proper See p105

University of British Columbia

A mix of historic and modern architecture, the buildings of BC's oldest university are complemented by diverse gardens. The campus offers fantastic views across the Strait of Georgia. At the renowned Museum of Anthropology *(see p34)*, visit the First Nations Longhouse, constructed in traditional Coast Salish style in 1993, to admire its four carved houseposts and two carved roof beam ends. The huge Pacific Spirit Regional Park *(see p88)* draws many visitors. Ⓢ *Map A2* • *604 822 2211* • *www.ubc.ca* • *First Nations Longhouse: 1985 West Mall*

Capilano Suspension Bridge Park

This North Vancouver park has been around since 1888. Its suspension bridge sways 230 ft (70 m) above the Capilano River *(see pp14–15)*.

Whistler

Two mountains, Whistler and Blackcomb, rise side by side at the resort town of Whistler. Enjoy views of the four villages and surrounding mountains and valleys year round, fog and snow allowing, by way of gondolas and lift chairs *(see pp28–31)*.

Modern fountain, Lonsdale Quay

North Vancouver

North Vancouver is a busy North Shore city of more than 46,000 residents. Take the scenic SeaBus ride across Burrard Inlet. Disembark at Lonsdale Quay, a public market selling fresh produce, meats, and baked goods, as well as handmade jewelry and crafts. Grab a takeaway from the food court and head for the outdoor seating area. Lynn Canyon Park boasts its own suspension bridge, spanning the dramatic canyon, 165 ft (50 m) above Lynn Creek, as well as 40 types of moss and 100-year-old Douglas firs. Stop in at the Ecology Centre to view the displays and films, and get details on park tours and trails. Ⓢ *Map B1* • *Lynn Canyon Park: at the end of Peters Rd, Lynn Valley* • *Lynn Canyon Ecology Centre: 604 990 3755*

Skier enjoying the view, Whistler Mountain

The Baden-Powell hiking trail stretches from Horseshoe Bay (see p86) to Deep Cove, and runs through Lynn Canyon Park

A Convocation of Eagles

Almost half the world's bald eagle population lives in BC. Thousands make their annual winter home in Brackendale. The first eagle count took place along the Squamish River in 1985, when six people counted 500 eagles. Some 2,000 eagles are now counted annually, feasting on spawning chum salmon and sitting in the cottonwood trees, with the best viewing in December and January. Brackendale Winter Eagle Festival takes place every January.

West Vancouver

This upscale North Shore community is home to over 42,000 people. Lighthouse Park (see p48), Cypress Provincial Park (see p48), and Horseshoe Bay are among the outdoor attractions here. Horseshoe Bay was once a popular summer spot for Vancouverites, who arrived by train or steamer, and it remains a pleasant day-trip destination. Its small bayside park features two totem poles and a pier. BC Ferries (see p106) depart here for Nanaimo, Bowen Island, and the Sunshine Coast. The pedestrian Centennial Seawall runs between Ambleside Park and charming Dundarave village. For a glimpse into the area's history, visit the West Vancouver Museum & Archives, which also has an interesting art collection. ◈ Map B1 • West Vancouver Museum & Archives: 680 17th St, 604 925 7295 • Open 11am–5pm Tue–Sat

Grouse Mountain

There's lots to do atop this Vancouver landmark including spotting wildlife and watching logging shows. The Feasthouse invites visitors into a beautifully crafted cedar longhouse to learn about Pacific Northwest First Nations cultures. At night, legends come alive with traditional Native cuisine, song, and dance. ◈ 6400 Nancy Greene Way, North Vancouver • Map F3 • 604 984 0661 • www. grousemountain.com • Adm to Skyride

Stanley Park

A 1.6 sq mile (4 sq km) park of tamed wilderness just outside downtown. The perimeter seawall has great views of the harbor and Coast Mountains (see pp8–11).

Steveston

Old-fashioned Steveston village was built on the salmon industry, with 15 canneries once employing thousands. The Gulf of Georgia Cannery National Historic Site offers a peek into this past. The converted 1894 building rests on pylons over the Fraser River. View the kid-friendly film inside, then tour the huge building. A children's discovery area is set up in the Ice House. ◈ Map B3 • Gulf of Georgia Cannery: 12138 4th Ave • 604 664 9009 • Closed Nov–Mar • Adm

The village of Steveston on the Fraser River

Brackendale

Brackendale is best known for the bald eagles that winter in the nearby 3-sq-mile (7.8-sq-km) Brackendale Eagles Provincial Park, but its ocean and river location also make this small town a great place for rafting and canoeing. After enjoying a day on the water in summer, or watching the eagles feast on salmon in winter, refuel in Brackendale Art Gallery's cozy teahouse.
🅢 Map E2 • Brackendale Art Gallery: 41950 Government Rd

The Stawamus Chief, Squamish

Squamish

"Squamish," a Coast Salish word meaning "mother of the wind," is an apt name for this windy town that has become a major center for outdoor activities. Rock climbers relish the challenge of the Stawamus Chief, an imposing granite monolith. Others windsurf on the Squamish River or camp in nearby parks, including renowned Garibaldi Provincial Park. Visit the West Coast Railway Heritage Park to see the famed black-and-gold Royal Hudson Steam Train or take a minitrain ride. 🅢 Map E3 • West Coast Railway Heritage Park: 39645 Government Rd • 1-604 898 9336 • Adm

A Drive Along the North Shore

Morning

🕐 Begin at the Stanley Park end of **Lions Gate Bridge**, where two stone lions will welcome you. Cross the bridge and take the North Vancouver exit onto Marine Drive, making the first left-hand turn onto Capilano Rd. Continue for 10 minutes to **Grouse Mountain**. Parking the car, hop on the Skyride for the 1-mile (1.5-km) ride to the top. Spend 90 minutes visiting the grizzlies at the **Refuge for Endangered Wildlife**, and watching the lumberjack show and **Theatre in the Sky**'s dramatic video on beautiful BC.

🍴 Lunch at **Altitudes Bistro**, enjoying marvelous views.

Afternoon

After lunch return to the car and drive down Capilano Rd, about 5 minutes, to **Capilano Suspension Bridge Park** (see pp14–15). Cross the heart-stopping bridge to **Treetops Adventure** for an eagle's-eye view of the rainforest.

Return to Marine Dr via Capilano Rd, driving west about 15 minutes to 25th St in West Vancouver, then turn left toward **Dundarave Park**. The scenic pier and park at the water's edge marks one end of the **Centennial Seawalk**.

After a breath of fresh sea air, walk up to **Marine Drive** and boutique shopping in Dundarave village.

End the day at one of **The Beach House**'s patio tables (see p90), watching the sun set over Dundarave Beach as you dine.

Brackendale Art Gallery hosts the village's annual eagle festival; call 1-604 898 3333 for details or visit www.brackendaleartgallery.com

87

Left **Pacific Spirit Regional Park** Right **VanDusen Botanical Gardens**

Best Greenspaces

1 Stanley Park
Stanley Park is replete with gardens, a seawalk, a rainforest with trails, and swimming pools. Rollerblades and bicycles can be rented near the Denman Street entrance to the park *(see pp8–11)*.

2 Pacific Spirit Regional Park
Trails in this 2.9-sq miles (7.5-sq km) park, also known as UBC Endowment Lands, are frequented by equestrians, walkers, and cyclists. They're well marked but can be rough going in bad weather. ® *W 16th Ave at Blanca St • Map A2 • 604 224 5739 • www.gvrd.bc.ca/parks*

3 Queen Elizabeth Park
This park at the highest point in Vancouver, 505 ft (167 m) above sea level, offers splendid views and gardens, and a conservatory *(see p38)*. ® *W 33rd Ave & Cambie St • Map B2 • 311 • www.vancouver.ca/parks*

4 VanDusen Botanical Garden
Secluded nooks and crannies can still be found at this world-famous garden. Seasonal displays. ® *5251 Oak St • Map B2 • 604 878 9274 • www.vandusengarden.org • Adm*

5 Grouse Mountain
Walk, bike, hike, snowboard, or ski up the mountain and enjoy a fantastic view of the city once you've reached the top. Challenge yourself with the 2-mile (3-km) Grouse Grind climb to the summit, at 3,973 ft (1,211 m) *(see p86)*.

6 Mount Seymour Provincial Park
Mountaineers and skiers relish the snow and gentle slopes in winter. In summer, hikers come seeking fabulous views. ® *1700 Mt Seymour Rd, North Vancouver • Map C1 • 604 986 2261 • www.mountseymour.com*

7 Cypress Provincial Park
Cypress Mountain offers sports galore and panoramic views as far as Mount Baker, in Washington State. ® *Top of Cypress Bowl Rd, West Vancouver • Map E3 • 604 926 5612 • www.cypressmountain.com*

8 George C. Reifel Migratory Bird Sanctuary
Snow geese and gyrfalcons are among the 60,000 birds visiting this huge site on Westham Island. View the wetlands from the platforms and hides. ® *5191 Robertson Rd • Map E4 • 604 946 6980 • www.reifelbirdsanctuary.com • Adm*

9 Lighthouse Park
Giant ferns and huge boulders are signatures of this waterfront park. Quiet trails lead through the area's last remaining stand of old-growth trees. ® *Marine Dr & Beacon Lane, West Vancouver • Map A1 • 604 925 7275 • www.westvancouver.net*

10 West Dyke Trail
This 3.5-mile (5.5-km) trail offers views of Sturgeon Banks, an estuary attracting 1.4 million birds a year as part of the Pacific Flyway. ® *Map A3 • www.richmond.ca/parksrec*

Many parks offer guided walking tours and electric cart tours; call ahead

Left **Mountain biker, Squamish area** Right **Whitewater rafting, Fraser River**

Adventure Sports

Glacier Skiing
Horstman Glacier *(see p28)* offers 0.2 sq miles (0.5 sq km) of skiing and incomparable views year-round. Varied terrain gives even experienced skiers plenty of thrills. ✆ *Whistler Blackcomb: 1 866 218 9690 • www.whistlerblackcomb.com*

Heli-Snowboarding
Fly away from the Whistler Blackcomb crowds into the pristine high-alpine powder. Guides help you choose from over 1,000 runs. ✆ *Great Canadian Adventure: 1 888 285 1676 • www.adventures.com*

Paragliding
Learn to be airborne on a tandem flight with a certified teacher. Coastal winds ensure breathtaking heights. ✆ *iParaglide: 604 681 4459 • www.iparaglide.com*

Rock Climbing
Squamish is one of the top climbing areas in North America. If you're not ready to tackle Stawamus Chief, a formidable cliff rising 2,139 ft (652 m), try Smoke Bluffs. ✆ *Squamish Rock Guides: 604 892 7816 • www.squamishrockguides.com*

Windsurfing
Windsurfers converge at the mouth of the Squamish River on Howe Sound, where north winds blow at 40 to 70 knots. Squamish Windsurfing Society operates the sailing park and rescue service, and charges a sailing fee. ✆ *www.squamishwindsurfing. org; Wind line: 604 892 2235*

Whitewater Rafting
Paddling or power rafting just two hours from Vancouver in Yale on the Nahatlatch, Thompson, and Fraser rivers. Choice of raft size, trip length, and fright factor. ✆ *Fraser River Raft Expeditions: 1 800 363 7238 • www.fraserraft.com*

Mountain Biking
BC offers unlimited trails and backroads. The 93-mile (150-km) Sea to Sky trail stretches from Squamish to D'Arcy. Find maps and trail ratings on the online Whistler Mountain Bike Guide. ✆ *www.whistlermountainbike.com*

Skydiving
Whether you're experienced or a newcomer to skydiving, the view of the Fraser Valley at 3,000 ft (915 m) is amazing. First-jump tandem lessons are on weekends and holidays. ✆ *Abbotsford Skydive Center: 604 854 3255 • www.vancouver-skydiving.bc.ca*

Diving
Find marine life, deep wall diving spots, a shipwreck, artificial reefs, and unusual geographic formations at Howe Sound's many dive sites. Charters, lessons, and equipment available. ✆ *The Diving Locker: 604 736 2681*

Kayaking with Orcas
Paddle alongside an orca pod at Vancouver Island's glacier-carved eastern coastline. ✆ *Ecomarine Paddlesport Centres: 604 689 7575 • www.ecomarine.com*

Left **Araxi** Right **Bishop's**

Restaurants

Bishop's
Chef John Bishop combines intimate dining with flawless service. Organic ingredients determine the weekly West Coast menu. Dinner only. ◈ *2183 W 4th Ave • Map B2 • 604 738 2025 • $$$$$*

Fraîche
Enjoy panoramic views from the West Vancouver mountainside while savoring delicious, award-winning cuisine that celebrates the west coast. ◈ *2240 Chippendale Rd • Map A1 • 604 925 7595 • $$$$*

Salmon House on the Hill
Perched in the North Shore hills, this restaurant is known for its green alderwood-grilled BC salmon. First Nations art and artifacts complement the rustic yet elegant interior of wood and glass. ◈ *2229 Folkstone Way, West Vancouver • Map B1 • 604 926 3212 • $$$$*

Siena
This casual, lively restaurant offers a menu of comfort-style Italian- and Spanish-influenced dishes with a focus on pasta and risotto. Head there early on Mondays when all wines are half price. ◈ *1485 W 12th Ave • Map B2 • 604 558 1485 • $$$*

Pear Tree
Widely considered to be the "Best of the Burbs", the Pear Tree feels world class. Its menu emphasizes fresh, high-quality ingredients. ◈ *4120 E Hastings St, Burnaby • Map C2 • 604 299 2772 • $$$$*

La Quercia
Named Restaurant of the Year by Vancouver Magazine, Vancouverites flock here for exceptional Italian dishes, exemplary service, and a great selection of Italian wines. ◈ *3689 West 4th Ave • Map B2 • 604 676 1007 • $$$*

The Beach House at Dundarave Pier
Sit on the deck of this 1912 house, choose a glass of wine from the long list, and enjoy West Coast cuisine. ◈ *150 25th St, West Vancouver • Map B1 • 604 922 1414 • $$$*

Araxi
Local produce is served with a Pacific Northwest bent at this vibrant, classy spot. Oysters and wild salmon for fish-lovers, lamb confit and steaks for others. Good wine list. ◈ *4222 Village Sq, Whistler • Map F1 • 604 932 4540 • $$$$$*

Trattoria Umberto
The warmth of Tuscany is reflected in the imaginative pasta dishes of celebrity chef Umberto Menghi. Other highlights include *cioppino* (Italian fish chowder) and *osso bucco* (braised veal shank). Excellent wine list. ◈ *4417 Sundial Pl, Whistler • Map F1 • 604 932 5858 • $$$$$*

Caramba!
This relaxed eatery encourages families to share wood-oven pizza, calamari, and rotisserie meats – try the chicken. ◈ *12–4314 Main St, Town Plaza, Whistler • Map F1 • 604 938 1879 • $$$$*

All restaurants accept credit cards and serve vegetarian food unless otherwise stated

Price Categories

For a three-course meal for one with half a bottle of wine (or equivalent meal), taxes and extra charges.	$ under $20
	$$ $20–$35
	$$$ $35–$60
	$$$$ $60–$85
	$$$$$ over $85

Above **Vij's**

🔟 Asian Restaurants

Jade Seafood Restaurant
One of the best Chinese restaurants in Vancouver, the chef here is a true master. Try the *dim sum* and crackling Peking duck. ◎ *8511 Alexandra Road • Map B3 • 604 249 0082 • $$$$*

Phnom Penh
Don't be fooled by the simple decor. Vancouverites line up here for the deep-fried squid and green papaya salad. ◎ *244 E Georgia St • Map M4 • 604 682 5777 • $$$*

Banana Leaf
Voted best Malaysian restaurant in the city for such dishes as fried whole crab with sambal sauce, and king prawns with peppercorns and garlic. ◎ *820 W Broadway • Map B2 • 604 731 6333 • $$$$*

Tojo's
Sushi chef Hidekazu Tojo welcomes you as warmly as he does the many celebrities who adore his cozy restaurant. Sidle up to the counter to watch this showman create delightful concoctions such as Dungeness crab topped with cherry blossoms, the shell serving as the plate. ◎ *1133 W Broadway • Map B2 • 604 872 8050 • $$$$$*

Kirin Seafood Restaurant
Enjoy Cantonese, Shanghai, and Szechuan dishes and award-winning *dim sum* at this restaurant popular with families. Excellent service. ◎ *Three West Centre, 7900 Westminster Hwy, Richmond • Map B3 • 604 303 8833 • $$$$*

Vij's
A symphony of wondrous flavors, the award-winning dishes are a West Coast adaptation of various Indian cooking styles. Specialties are curries, marinated lamb, short ribs, and duck. Dinner only. ◎ *1480 W 11th Ave • Map B2 • 604 736 6664 • $$$*

Sun Sui Wah
A stunning interior and an exciting *dim sum* selection. Alaska king crab and roast squab are notable entrées. Cantonese dishes are created with light, finely tuned flavors. ◎ *3888 Main St • Map B2 • 604 872 8822 • $$$*

Fisherman's Terrace
This local favorite boasts a large Cantonese menu and a grand dining room with chandeliers. ◎ *4151 Hazelbridge Way, Richmond • Map B3 • 604 303 9739 • $$$$*

Bao Bei
In Bao Bei's sophisticated dining room, a savvy take on Chinese home cooking is the order of the day, while one of the expertly composed cocktails makes a great way to start the evening. ◎ *163 Keefer St • Map M4 • 604 688 0876 • $$$$*

Hapa Izakaya
Imaginative Japanese tapas winning the hearts of locals and tourists alike. Contemporary combinations of sushi and sashimi and hot noodle dishes. ◎ *1479 Robson St • Map J3 • 604 689 4272 • $$$*

Following pages **The Fairmont Empress Hotel on Victoria's Inner Harbour**

Left **Legislative chamber, BC Parliament Buildings** Right **Entrance, Fairmont Empress Hotel**

Victoria

ICTURESQUE, PEACEFUL VICTORIA *is the perfect
getaway from bustling Vancouver. Known as the
City of Gardens, it boasts more than 3,000 hanging
baskets along its pretty streets. Established as a fort in
1843 by the Hudson's Bay trading company, Victoria
soon became a city of prestige and influence. It grew
up around Beacon Hill Park, created in 1858 by
Governor James Douglas. When Victoria became BC's
capital in 1868, the growing city attracted excellent
architects such as Francis Mawson Rattenbury. Today
the city buzzes around the Inner Harbour. Nearby is*

**Shrine detail, Art Gallery
of Greater Victoria**

*the oldest Chinatown in Western Canada, the Art Gallery of Greater
Victoria, and the home of Victoria's most famous artist, Emily Carr.*

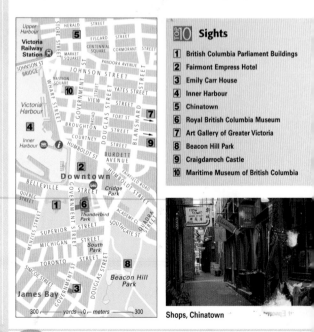

🔟 Sights

1. **British Columbia Parliament Buildings**
2. **Fairmont Empress Hotel**
3. **Emily Carr House**
4. **Inner Harbour**
5. **Chinatown**
6. **Royal British Columbia Museum**
7. **Art Gallery of Greater Victoria**
8. **Beacon Hill Park**
9. **Craigdarroch Castle**
10. **Maritime Museum of British Columbia**

Shops, Chinatown

British Columbia Parliament Buildings

Impressive, gray granite buildings house the provincial legislature. Overlooking the Inner Harbour, they were completed in 1898 by a newcomer, 25-year-old Francis Mawson Rattenbury from Leeds, England. At night, the Neo-classical structure is a wonderful sight, illuminated by 3,560 sparkling light bulbs. ✪ 501 Belleville St • Map N4–P4 • 250 387 3046 • Open 8:30am–5pm Mon–Fri • Guided tours • www.leg.bc.ca

Fairmont Empress Hotel

The luxury château-style landmark hotel (see p116) over-looking the Inner Harbour was designed by Rattenbury and built by the Canadian Pacific Railway in 1908. It is done up in grand style, with towering brick walls partially covered in ivy. The Crystal Ballroom shows off 18 crystal chandeliers and a mirrored ceiling. ✪ 721 Government St • Map P4 • 250 384 8111

Emily Carr House

Built in 1864, the Carr family home typifies the sensibilities of the Victorian era. The architecture has been described as both English Gingerbread and San Francisco Victorian, inspiring the

Emily Carr House

restoration of many of the area's old houses. Emily Carr, one of Canada's best-known artists and writers (see p19), was born here in 1871. Step into the formal dining room, parlor, and sitting room to see the Carrs' public face, reflecting everyday life, then relax with a cup of tea on the veranda. ✪ 207 Government St • Map P6 • 250 383 5843 • Open 11am–4pm Tue–Sat • Adm • www.emilycarr.com

Inner Harbour

The Inner Harbour is the historic center of Victoria. A mix of yachts, fishing boats, ferries, and float planes dock here, while pedestrians happily stroll along a wide, curved walkway. The harbor provides excellent views of the historic parliament buildings and the imposing Fairmont Empress Hotel. ✪ Map N3

Fairmont Empress Hotel, facing Inner Harbour

A Victoria Harbour Ferry trip is a wonderful way to see the sights. Visit www.harbourferry.com or call 250 708 0201

Governor James Douglas

James Douglas, known as the father of British Columbia, was born in Demerara, British Guiana (now Guyana), in 1803. His father was a Scottish merchant, his mother a free mulatto. Douglas married Amelia Connolly, the half-Native daughter of a fur trader. Working for the Hudson's Bay Company, Douglas established Fort Victoria in 1843. Over the next 20 years, Governor Douglas transformed Victoria into a center of political power, but he is best remembered as having established Beacon Hill Park, in 1858. Douglas retired in 1863. A knighthood followed. Sir James Douglas died in Victoria in 1877, at the age of 74.

5 Chinatown

Victoria's Chinatown once rivaled San Francisco's for size. Today it's an eclectic two-block area, signaled by the ornate Gate of Harmonious Interest. Chinatown was known as the Forbidden City by the European populace of the day. Once notorious Fan Tan Alley, said to be the narrowest street in Canada, hid gambling dens and a thriving opium industry. Today, restaurants, groceries, artists' studios, and souvenir shops fill the bustling streets of this designated heritage area. Ⓝ Fisgard & Herald sts at Government St • Map P1

Gate of Harmonious Interest, Chinatown

Gallery, Royal British Columbia Museum

6 Royal British Columbia Museum

Known for its Native artifacts and art, and displays highlighting BC history and natural wonders, the museum has excellent exhibits ranging from prehistory to the First Peoples Gallery. The IMAX Victoria Theatre and Thunderbird Park are also on the site (see pp24–5).

7 Art Gallery of Greater Victoria

Housed in an 1889 mansion, this gallery is known for its Asian collection, including a Shinto shrine in the Asian garden. Paintings and literary work by local artist Emily Carr (see p19) are another highlight. Ⓝ 1040 Moss St • 250 384 4171 • Open 10am–5pm daily (to 9pm Thu) • Adm

8 Beacon Hill Park

Noted for its gnarled Garry oak trees and 350-year-old Chinese bell, the park, dating from the mid-1800s, is a lovely place to stroll and picnic. Over 2,000 varieties of plants and trees, a rose garden, wooden bridges, and stream. Ⓝ Map Q6 • 250 361 0600

French Gothic tower, Craigdarroch Castle

9 Craigdarroch Castle

This four-story stone man-sion was built in the late 1880s for coal baron Robert Dunsmuir, who died soon after it was completed, leaving wife Joan and 11 children to squabble over the estate. Its 39 rooms each exude turn-of-the-19th-century elegance. Highlights include period furnishings, stained glass windows, a sandstone fireplace, and a grand white oak staircase. The views of the ocean and mountains from the tower are magnificent. ⊗ *1050 Joan Cres • 250 592 5323 • Open mid-Jun–Labour Day: 9am–7pm daily; Labour Day–mid-June: 10am–4:30pm daily • Adm*

10 Maritime Museum of British Columbia

Three floors of coastal history include the stories of the giant canoes of the Coast Salish First Peoples, the tall ships of the first European explorers, and pirate ships and whalers. Tumultuous tales of coastal shipwrecks are gruesomely fascinating. On the top floor is the former courtroom of notorious Matthew Baillie Begbie, known as the Hanging Judge. The 19th-century courtroom is preserved in all its glory. ⊗ *28 Bastion Sq • Map P2 • 250 385 4222 • Open 9:30–4:30pm daily • Adm*

Walking tour of Victoria

Morning

Starting at the corner of Wharf and Government, stroll 10 minutes north on **Government Street**. Shops along the way include some suitably British purveyors.

At Fisgard St, the colorful **Gate of Harmonious Interest** welcomes you to to **Chinatown**. Explore the area for an hour, dipping into tiny **Fan Tan Alley**, off Fisgard St. Continue west to Wharf St, then on to **Bastion Square**, the heart of **Old Town**, where fur traders boozed and brawled in the days of Fort Victoria.

The **Maritime Museum of British Columbia** is in a dignified former courthouse on the square. Devote an hour to its displays before heading to **Irish Times Pub**, 1200 Government St, for tasty fish and chips.

Afternoon

Admire the marine traffic from the **Inner Harbour** promenade. At the far end of the harbor, cross **Belleville Street** to the statue of a youthful Queen Victoria on the grounds of the **BC Parliament Buildings**. The fascinating **Royal British Columbia Museum** next door will take at least two hours to peruse.

Exit the museum on the east side to admire the totems in **Thunderbird Park** before checking out nearby historic Helmcken House. Cross Belleville St to the **Fairmont Empress Hotel** for a glimpse of the grandiose lobby.

Replenish with dinner or a drink at **Red Fish Blue Fish** on Broughton St Pier.

Left **Silk Road Aromatherapy & Tea Company** Right **Munro's Books**

Shopping

Philip Nyren
Also known as British Importers, this high-end shop features men's off-the-rack sportswear, suits, and accessories; also women's sportswear. ◈ *960 Yates St • Map R2 • 250 386 1496*

Smoking Lily
Vertical space in this closet-sized shop makes for unusual displays. T-shirts, scarves, bags, and more, all screen-printed by hand. ◈ *569a Johnson St • Map P2 • 250 382 5459*

Bernstein & Gold
Head to this lifestyle boutique for carefully chosen homewares, jewelry, footwear, and leather goods, as well as exclusive skincare brands and a spa. ◈ *608 Yates St • Map P2 • 250 384 7899*

Silk Road Aromatherapy & Tea Company
Silk Road offers a tea tasting bar similar to a wine bar. In addition to tea, it boasts a spa *(see p56)* and its own line of natural body care products. ◈ *1624 Government St • Map P1 • 250 704 2688*

She She Bags
Hundreds of purses crowd the shop: from glitzy clutch bags to industrial laptop bags. Check out She She Shoes across the street. ◈ *616 View St • Map P2 • 250 388 0613*

Rebel Rebel
At this unisex boutique mod meets boho-chic, from the runway to a rock show. Pieces by international designers and homegrown talent create a unique range of clothing, as well as an eclectic selection of shoes. ◈ *585 Johnson St • Map P2 • 250 380 0906*

Fan Tan Gallery
Gifts from around the world, with a focus on India, Indonesia, China, and France. Home accessories include mats, iron sconces, baskets, linens, bath products, art, and curios. ◈ *541 Fisgard St • Map P1 • 250 382 4424*

Violette Veldor
Inspired by quaint Paris jewelry boutiques, the owner stocks mainly Canadian-made pieces in both dainty and chunky styles. ◈ *1223 Government St • Map P2 • 250 388 7752*

Munro's Books
A magnificent store with a wide range of books from Canada, the US and the UK. ◈ *1108 Government St • Map P2 • 250 382 2464*

Fort Street Antiques
Discover one-of-a-kind silverware, glass and china, fine art, furniture, and jewelry on upper Fort St. ◈ *Fort St between Douglas St & Linden Ave • Map Q3*

LoJo (Lower Johnson) shopping area centered around Market Square boasts many locally-owned boutiques and stores

Price Categories

For a three-course meal for one with half a bottle of wine (or equivalent meal), taxes, and extra charges.

$	under $20
$$	$20–$35
$$$	$35–$60
$$$$	$60–$85
$$$$$	over $85

above **Empress Room, Fairmont Empress Hotel**

10 Restaurants & Cafés

1 Fairmont Empress Hotel
A variety of colonial-themed dining venues await at Victoria's grandest hotel. Especially popular is the formal afternoon tea, served daily since 1908 – reservations are required. ◈ 721 Government St • Map P4 • 250 384 8111 • $$$

2 Ulla
A small restaurant on the edge of Chinatown that serves impeccable American and international cuisine made with locally-sourced ingredients. Reservations recommended. ◈ 509 Fisgard St • Map P1 • 250 590 8795 • $$$$

3 Spinnakers Gastro Brewpub
Canada's oldest licensed brewpub's waterfront dining room menu includes all-natural smoked meats and sausages, perfect companions to the assortment of beers on tap. ◈ 308 Catherine St • 250 386 2739 • $$$

4 Canoe
Local organic produce, meat, and wild seafood are on offer at this brewpub, marina, and restaurant, in an historic 1894 waterfront property. Classics such as burgers and fries go especially well with a craft brew. ◈ 450 Swift St • Map N1 • 250 361 1940 • $$$

5 Brasserie L'École
French bistro dishes – lamb shank, mussels, and *frites* – using local products. ◈ 1715 Government St • Map P1 • 250 475 6260 • $$$

6 Red Fish Blue Fish
Set in a shipping container on the inner harbor, this canteen-style fish restaurant serves up sustainable seafood. ◈ 1006 Wharf St • Map P2 • 250 298 6877 • $$

7 Il Terrazzo Ristorante
Fine Northern Italian food; heated courtyard. Wood oven-roasted meats and pizzas, pastas, and seafood arrive with a flourish. ◈ 555 Johnson St • Map P2 • 250 361 0028 • $$$

8 Pagliacci's
Linguine, lasagna, and fettuccine are simple and satisfying. Pag's bread is coveted. ◈ 1011 Broad St • Map P3 • 250 386 1662 • $$$

9 The Noodle Box
Huge portions of noodle and rice dishes come in decorative boxes, at eight levels of spiciness. ◈ 818 Douglas St • Map P3 • 250 384 1314 • $

10 Wild Saffron Bistro
Progressive West Coast cuisine including fondues, rack of lamb, seafood, and vegetarian entrées. ◈ 506 Pandora Ave • Map P1 • 250 361 3310 • $$$

Left **Orca, Gulf Islands** Right **Mural depicting local history, Chemainus**

Excursions from Victoria

1 Nanaimo

The Old Quarter, built during the days when Nanaimo was a coal-mining town, has many 19th-century buildings, including the 1895 Nanaimo Court House. Stroll along the Harbourfront Walkway, stopping at The Bastion military museum. Nanaimo Downtown Farmers' Market is held next to Bastion on Fridays (May–Oct). Nanaimo is a good starting point for wildlife tours. ⊗ *Map D4*

2 Cowichan Valley

This pastoral valley is a mix of forests and farmland. Local wines, ciders, and gourmet cheeses attract gastronomically minded visitors by car and touring bicycles. Cowichan Lake is Vancouver Island's main fresh water lake and a terrific spot for swimming, canoeing, and fishing. The Cowichan River is a designated heritage treasure, famed for its fly fishing. ⊗ *Map D5*

Evergreen forests, Cowichan Valley

3 Chemainus

When the sawmill, the basis of its economy, closed in 1983, Chemainus transformed itself into a picturesque seaside town. More than 40 giant murals by local and international artists appear throughout the town, depicting the region's history. ⊗ *Map D5*

4 Gulf Islands

Visitors flock to these islands in the Strait of Georgia to enjoy their quietness and natural beauty. Salt Spring with its many artists' studios, and Galiano, which has a lovely provincial park, are the most popular island destinations. Saturna, Pender, Mayne, and Gabriola are the other major islands. Each has its own personality; all are accessible by BC Ferries from Swartz Bay *(see p107)*. ⊗ *Map E5*

5 Duncan

Duncan is known as the City of Totems for the 80 Coast Salish poles displayed around town. At the Quw'utsun' Cultural Centre see carvers at work, and some of the best Native arts and crafts in BC. The focus of the BC Forest Discovery Centre is the province's heyday of logging. In summer, a 1920s steam train carries passengers past heritage buildings and through a rainforest. ⊗ *Map E5*
• *Quw'utsun' Cultural Centre: 200 Cowichan Way • 250 746 8119 • Open Apr–Dec • BC Forest Discovery Centre: 2892 Drinkwater Rd • 250 715 1113 • Open summer: 10am–6pm daily; spring & fall: 10am–4pm daily • Adm*

For information about an excursion to the Long Beach area See pp26–7

Butchart Gardens

For over a century, the incomparable Butchart Gardens, wrung out of a worked-out quarry, have awed visitors with their lush and varied beauty *(see p38)*. ⊛ *800 Benvenuto Ave, Brentwood Bay • Map E5 • 250 652 5256 • Open Jun–Sep: 9am–10:30pm daily; otherwise closing times vary • Adm*

Broken Group Islands

An archipelago of some 100 rugged islands and islets is paradise for nature lovers, kayakers, and scuba divers. The area around Barkley Sound has outstanding views of coastal rainforest, beaches, and sea caves. Accessible only by boat, a guided tour is the best way to experience this isolated wilderness. Majestic Ocean Kayaking in Ucluelet offers whale watching and specialty tours. ⊛ *Map B5 • Majestic Ocean Kayaking: 250 726 2868 • Vancouver Island Kayak: 250 480 9409*

Parksville

Parksville's beautiful Rathtrevor Beach is easily accessible for waterside sports and activities. Dip your toes in the gentle surf, build sandcastles, dig clams, canoe, or camp along the 4 miles (7 km) of sand. Swim in the warmest saltwater north of California. Nearby are mini-golf courses, bistros, and art studios for one-of-a-kind souvenirs. ⊛ *Map C4*

Qualicum Beach

Beachcombers and kayakers find delightful Qualicum Beach and its nearby British-style village a pedestrian-friendly stopover. The curved beach presents magnificent sunsets. ⊛ *Map C4*

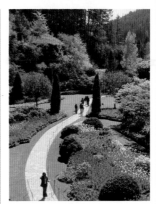

Victoria's Butchart Gardens

Goldstream Provincial Park

Massive old-growth Douglas firs, some 600 years old, tower overhead in this mystic rainforest only 12 miles (19 km) from Victoria. Once a fishing ground for the Coast Salish, miners overran the park during the Gold Rush of the late 1850s *(see p17)*. An annual fall salmon run on the Goldstream River attracts hundreds of majestic bald eagles. Dropping 155 ft (48 m) into a canyon pool, the park's waterfall is easily reached by a 5-minute walk along a trail. A visitor house offers a variety of weekend activities. ⊛ *Map E6 • Goldstream Nature House: 2930 Trans Canada Hwy • 250 478 9414 • Open 9am–4:30pm daily*

See Vancouver Island aboard the Malahat train, running from Victoria to Courtenay, and alight as often as you like; visit www.viarail.ca

101

Sockeye
Cooked Smoked Salmon
紅スモークサーモン
Tile Box 8oz (227g)
$32.75

Display

Display

Display

Salmon

Smoked Salmon

Sal...

Sockeye
Cooked Smoked Salmon
Wooden Box 16oz (454g)
$45.00

KWAKERE SALMON

CANADA

COOKED SMOKED SALMON

SOCKEYE
SALMON

COO

Sockeye
Cooked Smoked Salmon
紅スモークサーモン
Paper Box 16oz (454g)
$31.95

STREETSMART

VANCOUVER & VICTORIA'S TOP 10

Left **Winter skiing, Whistler Mountain** Right **Blooms of spring, Queen Elizabeth Park**

🔟 Planning Your Trip

When to Go
Vancouver and Victoria's temperate coastal climate is best from April to November. Rain falls intermittently from November to March. In the city and along the coast, winter temperatures rarely drop below freezing. Temperatures are lower in the mountains and, to the delight of skiers at resorts such as Whistler, there is snow. Summer can be hot but the nights are cooler.

What to Pack
Pack a warm sweater and a light jacket in late spring and early fall. In late fall and early spring, pack a heavier jacket or coat, and two warm sweaters. In winter, pack a hat, scarf, gloves, warm coat, and waterproof boots. A light sweater or blazer, cotton or linen dresses, slacks, shorts and T-shirts are ideal for summer; sunglasses, sunscreen, and an umbrella are a must.

Health Insurance
Unless your health insurance covers medical costs while traveling, buying comprehensive health and dental insurance is strongly recommended: Canada does not provide free medical services to visitors. Many credit card companies provide some degree of insurance; it is worthwhile to check this out before your trip.

Passports & Visas
A valid travel document, usually a passport, combined with a visa when needed, must be presented by visitors upon entry to Canada. Residents of many countries, such as the US, Australia, Ireland, New Zealand, and the majority of European countries, including Britain, do not need a visa. Visitors may remain in Canada for up to six months.

Customs
Canada's rules governing what can be brought into the country are complex. In general, do not bring live animals, fresh fruit, vegetables, meat, dairy products, plants, or firearms into Canada without first obtaining authorization. Limited amounts of alcohol and tobacco may be imported duty-free by visitors who are of age (19 and 18 years old, respectively). Upon entry into Canada, you must declare any cash amount equal to or more than Can$10,000.

Driver's License
Driver's licenses from the US and from other countries are valid in BC for up to six months. If you plan on staying longer, an International Driving Permit (obtained in your home country), combined with your license, will allow you to drive in the province for up to a year.

Car Insurance
Insurance coverage for drivers is mandatory in BC. If you are renting a car, check your policy before leaving home to see if it covers a rental car. Most rental agencies offer damage and liability insurance; it is a good idea to have both. Some credit cards include car insurance coverage.

Electricity
Canada uses a 110-volt, 60-cycle electrical system. Electrical sockets accept two- or three-pronged plugs. Bring a plug adapter and a voltage transformer to run appliances and cell-phone chargers that are not manufactured in North America or that don't have an optional voltage switch.

Time Zone
Vancouver is in the Pacific Time zone (eight hours behind Greenwich Mean Time). Daylight Savings Time begins the first Sunday in April when clocks are turned forward one hour, and ends in late October when clocks are turned back one hour.

Discounts
Most movie theaters, major attractions, and public transit systems offer reduced rates for people over age 65. Students are eligible for many discounts with ID. Hotels also often offer discounts, but only if you ask for them.

Contact the Canadian embassy or High Commission nearest you for entry requirements, or visit www.migrationexpert.com/canad

Left **Downtown crowds** Right **Pre-paid parking area**

ᵀᴼᴾ10 Things to Avoid

1 Leaving Valuables in Cars

Vancouver is notorious for thefts from cars. Leave nothing visible in your vehicle and take all valuables with you, including documents. If you shop, don't assume putting purchases in your car's trunk will keep them safe: thieves may spot you storing bags in the trunk and steal them when you continue shopping.

2 Hotel Telephone Calls

Avoid making long-distance calls from your hotel room that are charged directly to hotel bills – they are at least three times more expensive than using a phone card. You can buy a pre-paid phone card at convenience stores and newsstands. Local calls may be free from your room, or there may be a charge. Ask before you call out as this can add up.

3 Rush Hour

The best way to deal with rush hour traffic in Vancouver is to avoid it entirely. From 3:30pm to 6:00pm traffic slows or even comes to a complete halt. In the morning, wait until 9:30am before driving. Don't underestimate your driving time. Rush hour in Victoria is lighter.

4 Driving in Cities

Since many attractions in Vancouver and Victoria are within walking distance, or are an easy bus ride away, it makes sense to leave your car at the hotel. If you are thinking of renting a vehicle to travel further afield, check the alternatives first, such as public transit, which even offers shuttle buses to Whistler in ski season *(see p107)*.

5 Tickets

Obey the speed limits posted on city streets. Speeding tickets are costly in BC. In pre-paid parking areas, make sure to buy ample time. Parking tickets come swiftly and are an unwelcome drain on your budget.

6 Pickpockets

A pickpocket looks just like any other person, so be watchful of people bumping into you – it could be a thief at work. A favorite trick of pickpockets is to work the crowds during the area's many festivals so be particularly careful at these events. Bus stops are notorious. Keep your valuables close to your body under your outer garments *(see p111)*.

7 Dangerous Areas

Vancouver is generally a safe city but as with any big city, caution is advised. The Theatre District downtown can be the scene of rowdy behavior. The downtown eastside around Hastings and Main streets, and west on Hastings from Main to Cambie, is known for drug dealers. Take a bus or taxi to and from Chinatown along Pender Street to avoid this section. Finally, avoid all parks after dark. Crime rates in Victoria are low, though panhandlers may prove a nuisance.

8 Airport Con Artists

Disoriented travelers are easy targets for con artists and thieves. Never travel with large amounts of money or precious jewelry. Avoid taxi drivers who walk up to you offering a ride; take a licensed cab at the taxi stand or a limousine with set rates.

9 Panhandlers

Panhandlers face legal restrictions in BC, but many still appear in various locales. At stoplights, some offer to wash windshields for money. The cities of Vancouver and Victoria discourage giving money to panhandlers.

10 Prostitutes

Prostitutes of both sexes ply their trade in Vancouver, especially in the downtown eastside. Often they are working to support a drug habit and are at a higher risk of being infected with HIV/AIDS than is the general population. The city is trying to improve the lives of prostitutes, and to better control prostitution, but their number remains high.

If you are cycling around Vancouver or Victoria, make sure to lock your bike securely when you take a break

Streetsmart

Left **Airplane taking off from Vancouver Airport** Right **Traffic, downtown Vancouver**

Arriving in Vancouver & Victoria

Main Airports
Vancouver's international airport has two terminals, one for Canadian destinations, one for international. Victoria's airport has one terminal. Free baggage carts are available at both airports.
◉ *Vancouver Airport info: 604 207 7077, www.yvr. com • Victoria Airport info: 250 953 7500, www. victoriaairport.com*

Immigration
Cards to be filled out for immigration and customs are distributed on international flights. On arrival, the immigration officer will ask to see your passport or other ID.

Connections from Vancouver International Airport
Vancouver airport is 15 miles (24 km) south of downtown Vancouver. Canada Line whisks passengers to downtown Vancouver and Richmond with several stops in between. Public buses, taxis, limousines, and car rentals are also available. The Airporter express bus departs every 15 minutes for major Vancouver hotels, the cruise ship terminal (see p12), and the intercity bus depot. The No. 424 bus picks up on Level 1 of the domestic terminal for Airport Station, by the Delta Hotel. From there, buses go to Vancouver, Richmond, and beyond.
◉ *Airporter bus: 1 800 668 3141 • Canada Line: 604*
247 5757, www.protransbc. com • TransLink: 604 946 8866, www.translink.bc.ca

Connections from Victoria International Airport
Located 14 miles (22 km) north of Victoria, the airport is serviced by public transit (route No. 70), taxis, limousines, and cars for hire. The AKAL Airport Shuttle departs every 30 minutes for major Victoria hotels.
◉ *Victoria Regional Transit: 250 382 6161 • AKAL Shuttle: 250 386 2525*

Car Rental
At Vancouver airport, most car rental companies have booths on the ground floor of the airport parking garage. If you are driving downtown, note that a section of Granville Street is closed to private vehicles; signs direct you to side streets. Victoria's airport is serviced by several car rental companies.

Long-Distance Buses
Greyhound buses arrive from the US and elsewhere in Canada at Pacific Central Station (1150 Station St, Vancouver).
◉ *Greyhound: 1 800 661 8747 • www.greyhound.ca*

Flights from Downtown Vancouver
From the tiny Coal Harbour Airport, West Coast Air links Vancouver to Victoria and Nanaimo. Harbour Air
Seaplanes services the Gulf Islands and HeliJet operates a daily service to Victoria.
◉ *West Coast Air & Harbour Air: 604 606 6888 • HeliJet International: 1 800 665 4354*

By Rail
Trains arrive at Pacific Central Station in Vancouver, at 1150 Station St. VIA Rail trains arrive from points in Canada. Amtrak's Cascades route links Eugene and Portland, Oregon, and Seattle, Washington, to Vancouver with daily trains.
◉ *VIA Rail: 1 888 842 7245, www.viarail.ca • Amtrak: 1 800 872 7245, www.amtrak.com*

By Water
Ferry services link Seattle with Vancouver and Victoria and BC Ferries connects Vancouver with Victoria, the Gulf Islands, and Nanaimo. Cruise ships dock at Canada Place (see p61). Pleasure boats dock at the many marinas; call Tourism BC for details.
◉ *BC Ferries: 1 888 223 3779, www.bcferries.com • Tourism BC: 1 800 435 5622, www.hellobc.com*

By Road
Washington state's I-5 connects with Hwy 99 at the BC border; this leads to Vancouver and Whistler. BC's main Canada-US border crossing is the International Peace Arch in Blaine, Washington.

Vancouver and BC bus schedules are available for free at Vancouver airport's customer service counters, Arrivals level

Left **Vancouver's SkyTrain** Right **Taxi in front of the Opus Hotel, Vancouver**

🔟 Getting Around Vancover & Victoria

Buses & SeaBus
Public transit (Translink) bus routes extend across Greater Vancouver. Ask the driver for a transfer so you can switch to the SkyTrain or SeaBus – catamarans that cross the harbor in a short 12 minutes. The Victoria Regional Transit System operates a large network of buses across Victoria. ❧ *Vancouver route info: 604 953 3333 • www. translink.bc.ca • Victoria route info: 250 382 6161*

SkyTrain
Vancouver's SkyTrain is mainly an above-ground light rapid transit system. It also includes Canada Line, which has 16 stations and connects downtown to Vancouver International Airport and Richmond. Tickets are also transfers. They are good for 90 minutes, and valid for round trips and connections to buses and the SeaBus.

Transit Fares
Vancouver's TransLink system has three fare zones, but on weekdays after 6:30pm and weekends, the system reverts to one zone. Victoria's transit system has two fare zones. In both cities, bus drivers do not sell tickets or provide change. If you don't have a ticket, pay the exact cash fare when boarding. Sheets or books of 10 tickets and day passes are money-savers. These are sold at SkyTrain stations (Vancouver) and at many convenience stores and supermarkets. People with disabilities, children 5 to 13 years, seniors and students with proper ID are eligible for concession fares. Children under 4 years ride free in Vancouver, under 6 in Victoria.

Taxis
Flagging a taxi on Vancouver city streets is easy – cabs are plentiful. In Victoria, fewer taxis cruise the streets, so it is best to order a cab by phone.

Ferries
Ferries to Victoria and the Gulf Islands depart from Tsawwassen; those to Nanaimo, the Sunshine Coast, and Bowen Island leave from Horseshoe Bay. All ferries carry bicycles for a fee. Car reservations are advised for peak periods. ❧ *Ferry info: 1 888 223 3779 in BC; 250 386 3431 outside BC • www.bcferries.com*

Walking
Walking is the best way to explore downtown Vancouver and Victoria. Streets are fairly safe (see p105). The south arm of the False Creek seawalk (see p71) leads from Vanier Park (see p78) past several beaches to Spanish Banks, UBC (see p85), and beyond. In Victoria, a walk on the Inner Harbour promenade offers views of historic buildings and the harbor (see p95).

HandyDART
Both Victoria and Vancouver operate a shared-ride service for people unable to use public transit. Pre-register at least 10 days ahead of your trip. ❧ *HandyDART: Vancouver, 604 430 2692, Victoria: 250 727 9607*

Cycling
Cyclists must follow the same rules of the road as drivers. Bikes may not be ridden on sidewalks, and wearing a helmet is mandatory. Bikes are allowed on Vancouver's SkyTrain and SeaBus in non-peak hours. Buses in both cities offer bike racks on many routes.

Driving
A good map is essential, especially in Vancouver. Hwys 1 and 99 can be very busy during rush hour (see p105). There are no freeways by-passing the city core. Speed limits are posted. Right-hand turns on red lights are legal throughout BC unless otherwise posted.

Boat Tours
For boat tours of Howe Sound and Victoria Harbour, check with the tourist information centers in Vancouver and Victoria. ❧ *Touristinfo Centre Vancouver: Plaza Level, 200 Burrard St, 604 683 2000, www. tourismvancouver.com • Tourism Victoria: 812 Wharf St, 250 953-2033, www.tourismvictoria.com*

For Vancouver public transit information, call 604 953 3333. For Victoria public transit information, call 250 382 6161

107

Left **Free outdoor activities, English Bay** Right **Inexpensive cruise, SeaBus ferry**

TOP 10 Budget Tips

1 Attractions Discounts

Save up to 40 percent on tickets to popular Vancouver attractions by buying tickets in advance from the Tourism Vancouver Visitor Centre. In Victoria, discount coupon books are available at Tourism Victoria. ◈ *Vancouver: 200 Burrard St, 604 683 2000 • Victoria: 31 Bastion Sq, 250 414 6999*

2 Budget Shopping

Look for inexpensive, unusual souvenirs in Chinatown and in the shops along Commercial Drive *(see p55)*, brimming with ethnic goods. Visit Main Street for second-hand bargains and one-of-a-kind designer wear on a budget. In Victoria, you can spend hours browsing through the collectibles at the Capital Iron (1900 Store St), then stop next door at Value Village (1810 Store St) for rock-bottom prices on used clothing and housewares.

3 Savings on the Go

Save on public transit costs in Vancouver and Victoria by buying all-zone day passes, or books of ten tickets for the price of eight *(see p107)*.

4 Outdoor Activities

Vancouver and Victoria's year-round mild weather makes outdoor activities especially appealing. From a stroll along Stanley Park's paths *(see pp8–9)* to the tough

Grouse Grind climb *(see p88)*, Vancouver has hiking trails for all fitness levels. Or rent a bike, buy a kite, or grab your binoculars and birder's guide and head to the beach. In Victoria, the Inner Harbour walkway *(see p95)* provides free entertainment and exercise.

5 Free Festivals

Vancouver and its surrounds host plenty of free events during the summer months, such as Canada Day with its live music, parade, and fireworks display at Granville Island *(see pp20–21)*. For foodies, there are food festivals galore year-round. Check out the Georgia Straight (www.straight.com) and www.tourismvancouver.com for upcoming festivities.

6 Free or Reduced Admission Days

Admission to the Vancouver Art Gallery *(see pp18–19)* is by donation on Thursdays, from 5 to 9pm. UBC Museum of Anthropology *(see p34)* is free Tuesdays after 5pm. The BC Parliament Buildings in Victoria *(see p95)* offer free guided tours from late May to September.

7 Show Discounts

Tickets Tonight sells half-price tickets at the Touristinfo Centre for Vancouver shows the day of the performance. Some theaters offer two-for-one tickets to matinees and

previews; be sure to ask. Vancouver Playhouse *(see p42)* sells discount tickets one hour before show time. The Victoria Symphony offers ticket discounts with a receipt from certain restaurants. ◈ *Tourism Vancouver Visitor Centre: 200 Burrard St, 604 683 2000 • Victoria Symphony, 250 385 6515*

8 Cut-Rate Cruises

Rides on BC Ferries are inexpensive mini-cruises. Particularly lovely is the route to the southern Gulf Islands. In Vancouver, if you have only an hour to spare, hop on the SeaBus or any False Creek ferry *(see p107)*. ◈ *BC Ferries: 1 888 223 3779 • www.bcferries.bc.ca*

9 Cheap Eats

It's easy to find good-quality but bargain Asian food in Vancouver. In Victoria, head to Chinatown for deals. Or buy a pulled pork sandwich, *dim sum*, or halibut cone from one of the food carts on Vancouver's city streets.

10 Campus Deals

Both Simon Fraser University and the University of British Columbia *(see p85)* put on free or inexpensive concerts, lectures, and other events. Admission is cheap to Cinecenta's second-run movies, at the University of Victoria. Visit the websites for listings. ◈ *www.sfu.ca • www.ubc.ca • www.cinecenta.com*

In summer, the Architectural Institute of BC offers walking tours of Victoria and Vancouver for $5; call 604 683 8588 or visit www.aibc.ca

Left **Vancouver Trolley tour** Right **Tourism Vancouver Visitor Centre**

TOP10 Excursion Tips

1 Walking Tours
Learn more about Vancouver's Chinatown with guides from the Chinese Cultural Centre. Historic Gastown comes alive in Gastown Business Improvement Society (GBIS) tours. Walkabout Historic Vancouver has professional guides who lead tours of downtown, Granville Island, and Gastown. ⊗ *Chinese Cultural Centre: 604 658 8880 • GBIS: 604 683 5650 • Walkabout Historic Vancouver: 604 720 0006*

2 Trolley Tours
Classic trolley cars are replicated in modern sightseeing buses. The year-round city tour is two hours, but you can hop on or off at any of the 23 stops. ⊗ *Vancouver Trolley: 604 801 5515*

3 Rail Tours
Rail travel is a Canadian classic. VIA Rail transcontinental service guarantees cozy sleepers, fine cuisine, and attentive staff. Rocky Mountaineer Vacations offers spectacular packages, such as a famed two-day, all daylight trip between Vancouver and the Rockies. ⊗ *Rocky Mountaineer Vacations: 604 606 7245 or 1 800 665 7245 • VIA Rail: 1 888 842 7245*

4 Bus Tours
Pacific Coach Lines offer various day trips, including a Victoria City Tour and Butchart Gardens en route to Vancouver. Tours include pick-ups and drop-offs from select hotels. West Coast City & Nature Sightseeing has a daily shuttle to Whistler and provides mini-coach tours with a focus on natural sights. ⊗ *Pacific Coach Lines: 1 800 661 1725 • www.pacificcoach.com • West Coast City & Nature Sightseeing: 604 451 1600*

5 First Nations Tours
Coast Salish guides lead two-hour interpretive paddles in a 12-passenger, traditional-style, ocean-going canoe. The protected waters of Burrard Inlet are the background for stories and songs that capture the rich culture of Northwest Coast First Nations. Kayaking is an alternative. All ages welcome, from May to October. ⊗ *Takaya Tours: 604 904 7410*

6 Whale Watches
For sightings of orcas (killer whales), Dall's porpoises, seals, and other wildlife, Wild Whales Vancouver departs the harbor for the Gulf of Georgia and beyond. Vancouver Whale Watch has Zodiac-style boats with on-board naturalists. Steveston Seabreeze Adventures runs from the Fraser River to the Gulf Islands on larger vessels. ⊗ *Steveston Seabreeze Adventures: 604 272 7200 • Vancouver Whale Watch: 604 274 9565 • Wild Whales Vancouver: 604 699 2011*

7 Horse-Drawn Tours
Traditional horse-drawn narrated tours of Stanley Park run March to November, taking up to 20 passengers per trolley. One-hour tours of Victoria visit Beacon Hill Park and other scenic spots. ⊗ *Stanley Park Horse-Drawn Tours: 604 681 5115 • www.stanleyparktours. com • Victoria Carriage Tours: 1 877 663 2207*

8 Cycle Tours
Local guides oversee cycling, mountain biking, and multi-sport adventures. Gourmet meals, a stop at the hot springs, and luxurious support van included. Small groups. ⊗ *Rocky Mountain Cycle Tours: 604 898 8488 or 1 800 661 2453 • www. rockymountaincycle.com*

9 Golf in Whistler
Let Golf Whistler plan your accommodation, transportation, and tee times at Whistler's four championship golf courses. All you have to do is play. ⊗ *Golf Whistler: 1 866 723 2747 • www.golfwhistler.com*

10 Rafting Trips
Whitewater rafting expeditions on the mighty Fraser, Thompson, and Nahatlatch rivers, from one to six days in length, are suited to various experience levels. Camp or enjoy B&B accommodations at the Yale base. ⊗ *Fraser River Raft Expeditions: 1 800 363 7238*

Left **Telephone booth sign** Middle **Tickets Tonight sign** Right **Wheelchair access sign**

Useful Information

Media
The two largest newspapers in BC are produced in Vancouver, the *Vancouver Sun* and the *Vancouver Province*. The two national newspapers, the *Globe and Mail* and the *National Post*, are also available. Popular radio stations include CBC Radio Two (FM 105.7) for classical music, NEWS 1130 (AM 1130) for news, The FOX (FM 99.3) for rock music, and QMFM (FM103.5) for easy-listening music. The most popular Canadian TV stations are CBC, CTV, Global, Bravo, CityTV, and, in BC, the Knowledge Network.

Entertainment Listings
Georgia Straight, a weekly Vancouver tabloid, is available free at cafés, bars, bookshops, libraries, and street boxes. It is the best source to check the local music and art scene. For same-day savings on tickets to many events and performances, try Tickets Tonight at the Burrard St Tourist Infocentre *(see p108)*. ✆ www.straight.com

Currency
The Canadian unit of currency is the dollar, which is divided into 100 cents. Coins come in denominations of 1, 5, 10, and 25 cents, and 1 and 2 dollars. Bank notes (bills) come in denominations of $5, $10, $20, $50, $100, and $500. Plan to arrive with at least $100 in local currency and get change on arrival for tipping and transit (when traveling on buses you will need to pay the driver the exact fare in cash if you haven't bought a ticket in advance).

Taxes
In Canada, taxes are not included in the listed price unless specified, so when making a purchase add a further 12 percent for HST (Harmonized Sales Tax). An additional 2 percent MRDT (Municipal and Regional District Tax) may also be charged on accommodation.

Websites
Helpful information for planning your trip to Vancouver, Victoria, and Whistler is available online. ✆ www.vancouver.ca • www.tourism vancouver.com
• www.tourismvictoria.com
• www.tourismwhistler.com

Telephones
Public telephones are often both coin- and card-operated. Local calls cost $0.50; directory assistance (411) is about $1. Most convenience stores sell phone cards. Within Greater Vancouver, you must prefix the local telephone number with area code 604. Long-distance calls in BC require either a 604 or 250 prefix. For a long-distance number in North America, dial the prefix 1 and then the area code. To dial abroad, dial 011 + country code + city code (dropping the first 0).

Public Holidays
New Year's Day (Jan 1), Family Day (BC, early Feb), Good Friday and Easter Monday (Mar or Apr), Victoria Day (usually 3rd Mon in May), Canada Day (Jul 1), BC Day (1st Mon in Aug), Labour Day (1st Mon in Sep), Thanksgiving (2nd Mon in Oct), Christmas Day (Dec 25), Boxing Day (Dec 26). Remembrance Day (Nov 11) is a holiday for banks and government offices.

Accessibility
Vancouver and Victoria work hard to make their attractions and services accessible but it is best to check ahead. In Vancouver, SeaBus and SkyTrain are accessible, and all SkyTrain stations have elevators. Lift and "kneeling" public transit buses for people with mobility aids operate on many routes in both cities *(see p107)*.

Consulates
In emergencies, your consulate may be of assistance. ✆ UK: 800-1111 Melville St, 604 683 4421
• USA: 1095 W Pender St, 604 685 4311

Drinking
The legal drinking age in BC is 19. Consuming alcoholic beverages in public spaces is not allowed.

Left **Hospital sign** Middle **Police car** Right **No smoking zone**

🔟 Security & Health

1 Hotel Room Safety
When you've checked into your room, look on the back of the entrance door for a map showing the escape route to take in case of fire. Always leave the security latch in place when in your room and don't admit strangers. Some hotels have floors just for women – ask when booking, if you are a woman traveling alone.

2 Food Safety
City health officials inspect most Vancouver and Victoria food establishments, including pubs and delicatessens, regularly. Reports may be viewed online. 🔍 www.foodinspectionweb.vcha.ca

3 Emergency Help
Various emergency and helplines are available to call in a crisis. 🔍 Emergency and ambulance: 911 • Vancouver Police Department: 604 717 3321 • Victoria Police Department: 250 995 7654 • BC Nurseline: 604 215 4700 • VictimLINK: 1 800 563 0808

4 Public Transit
Skytrain (including Canada Line) platforms provide designated waiting areas in Vancouver; these are recommended at night. Available on most Victoria and Vancouver buses and some regional buses in BC, Request Stop allows a woman to get off a bus at locations between regular stops. Tell the driver at least one stop ahead of where you want to get off, and leave the bus by the front doors. The rear doors will remain closed so that no one can follow you off.

5 Know Your Surroundings
Carry a good map with you and check out the route to and from your destination before starting out. If you plan on returning late, make sure you have enough change and cash to call for and pay for a taxi. Avoid dark places such as parks and alleyways at night, especially if you are on your own, and avoid known danger spots *(see p105)*.

6 Hospital Emergency Rooms
Emergency treatment is available 24 hours a day. 🔍 Vancouver: Children's Hospital, 4500 Oak St, 604 875 2000; Lion's Gate Hospital, 231 E 15th St, 604 988 3131; St Paul's Hospital, 1081 Burrard St, 604 682 2344; Vancouver General, 899 West 12th Ave, 604 875 4111
• Victoria: Royal Jubilee Hospital, 1900 Fort St, 250 370 8000; Victoria General Hospital, 1 Hospital Way, 250 727 4212

7 Dental Emergencies
The BC Dental Association can link you with a nearby dentist during regular office hours. After office hours, go to a hospital emergency room. 🔍 British Columbia Dental Association • 604 736 7202

8 Smoking
Vancouver is a smoke-free city and smoking is not allowed in public spaces, including parks and beaches, or in workplaces.

9 Pharmacies
The majority of pharmacies in Vancouver and Victoria are open from 9am to 9 or 10pm. Some are open later. There are three 24-hour Shoppers Drug Mart pharmacies in Vancouver. The most central is on Davie Street.
🔍 Vancouver: Shoppers Drug Mart, 1125 Davie St, 604 669 2424 • Victoria: London Drugs, 911 Yates St, 250 360 0880

10 Theft Prevention
To help prevent theft don't flash cash around. Your wallet or valuables should be stored close to your body, not in your backpack, back pocket, or belt-pack, where they can be easily pilfered. If you carry a purse, ensure it closes tightly. When leaving your hotel room – even just for a short time – first lock up valuables and important documents in your room's safe, if it has one. If it doesn't, have them put in the hotel's safe.

Left **Georgia Street rotunda, Pacific Centre** Right **Backpackers Shop**

🔟 Shopping Tips

1 Store Hours
Most shops are open 10am to 6pm, Monday to Saturday (often later on Thursday). Department stores and shops in malls and retail districts may stay open to 9pm, Monday to Saturday, and open Sunday from 11am or noon to 5pm. Many shops close January 1, July 1, Labour Day, Thanksgiving and December 25.

2 Payment
MasterCard, American Express, and Visa credit cards are widely accepted, Diner's Club and Discovery less so. Debit cards compatible with Plus, Interac, or Cirrus systems are also widely accepted. You will need your PIN.

3 Sales & Returns
Excellent savings are to be had on Boxing Day (December 26). Sale items and sometimes those at full price may not be refundable, or exchangeable only. Be sure to ask about the return policy.

4 Department Stores
Vancouver's department store, The Bay in the Pacific Centre, carries practically everything. Holt Renfrew sells high-end clothing and accessories. The Bay also anchors Victoria's Bay Centre, which is the premier shopping destination in downtown Victoria. ◈ Holt Renfrew: 737 Dunsmuir St • Map K3

• The Bay: 647 Granville St, Vancouver • Map K3
• The Bay: 1150 Douglas St, Victoria • Map P2

5 Shopping Malls
The largest downtown mall is Pacific Centre (see p55). Other malls include Sinclair Centre (see p54), and Metrotown (see p55). Victoria's Bay Centre has over 80 shops. Market Square's shops are in heritage buildings. ◈ Bay Centre: 1150 Douglas St • Map P2 • Market Square: 560 Johnson St • Map P2

6 Music
HMV has the city's largest range of CDs and DVDs. Classical and jazz lovers should head to the Magic Flute. For vinyl, try Neptoon Records. Lyle's Place in Victoria sells new and used CDs, from jazz to punk rock. ◈ HMV: 788 Burrard St at Robson St • Map J3 • Magic Flute: 2203 W 4th Ave • Map B2 • Neptoon Records: 3561 Main St • Map B2 • Lyle's Place: 770 Yates St • Map Q2

7 Books
Chapters has a good selection and several locations. Used-book seller MacLeod's specializes in Canadiana and history. Visit Duthie Books for contemporary literature, and Kidsbooks for children's titles. Munro's of Victoria sells a range of titles. ◈ Chapters: 788 Robson St • Map K4 • Duthie Books: 2239 W 4th Ave • Map B2 • Kidsbooks:

3083 W Broadway • Map A2 • MacLeod's: 455 W Pender St • Map L3 • Munro's: 1108 Government St • Map P2

8 Alcohol
Alcohol sales are restricted to BC government Liquor Stores (wine, spirits, and beer), private wine sellers, Vintners Quality Assurance (VQA) outlets (specializing in BC wines), and Cold Beer Stores. ◈ Liquor Store: 1120 Alberni St • Map J3 • Village VQA Wines: 3536 W 41st Ave • Map A2 • Wine Barrel: 644 Broughton St, Victoria • Map P3

9 Convenience Stores
Small shops selling cigarettes, toiletries, cold drinks, snacks, and lottery tickets are ubiquitous in Vancouver and Victoria. Some also sell public transit tickets.

10 Souvenirs
Pick up a few local souvenirs to remind you of your time in Vancouver or Victoria. How about some salmon candy (salmon cured in maple syrup) for a last-minute buy at Vancouver Airport, a blown glass bauble or bottle of craft sake from Granville Island's public market (see p80), or a First Nations bentwood box from Coastal Peoples Fine Art Gallery in Vancouver. ◈ Coastal Peoples Fine Art Gallery: 1024 Mainland St • Map K5

Groceries, newspapers, magazines, and bicycles are exempt from the 7 percent PST (Provincial Services Tax)

Left **Bedroom, Pacific Palisades Hotel** Left **Wines, Don Francesco restaurant**

🔟 Accommodation & Dining Tips

Hotel Taxes
In BC, accommodation is taxed with 8 percent provincial hotel room tax. Some properties are also required to add an additional 2 percent tourism tax on hotel rooms in Vancouver, Victoria, and Whistler.

Rooms
Most hotel rooms are well furnished and of a good size. Most have two double beds or one queen- or king-sized bed; twin-bedded rooms may also be available. If you are sensitive to noise, ask for a room away from the elevator and the ice and dispensing machines. About 85 percent of rooms in Vancouver, Victoria, and Whistler are smoke-free.

Rack Rates
Hotel rates vary according to the hotel category, the day of week, and season. Peak rates are weekdays and from April to December. Rack rates, the basic room rates, are the ones used in this book to provide a guide price. It is usually possible to get a better deal, especially if you are booking online. Discounts are often available to seniors, members of clubs such as auto associations, or the Elderhostel. When booking, ask what special rates apply and remember to bring proof of membership with you.

Concierges
Mid- and large-size hotels have concierges on staff whose job it is to cater to the needs and whims of the guests. They will procure tickets to shows and sports games, make restaurant reservations, arrange transportation, and offer helpful tips.

Extra Costs
Parking at downtown hotels can be costly, so inquire about rates (taxes also apply). Some hotels do offer free parking. Telephone calls made from your room phone can be pricey, as are drinks and snacks consumed from the room's minibar. These costs can add up quickly, and will appear on your final room bill.

Restaurant Reservations
Most restaurants take reservations. It's a good idea to book a table at a popular dining spot on arriving or even in advance of your trip. Mention if you have special needs or dietary requirements. It is considered good form to cancel your reservation if your plans change.

Tipping
Tips and service charges are not usually added to dining bills, though they may be if your party consists of six people or more. For service at restaurants, cafés, and clubs, plan on tipping about 15 percent of the pre-tax amount. An easy way of estimating the tip is to add up the taxes on the bill. At bars, leave a dollar or two for the bartender. Tip porters and bellhops at least $1 per bag or suitcase; cloakroom attendants $1 per garment and chambermaids, about $5 per day. A hotel doorman will also appreciate a dollar or two for his services.

Dress Codes
Jacket and tie are almost never required in restaurants, though many diners opt to wear them on a special evening out, especially to an upscale place. Some clubs, however, may not allow you in if you are wearing sneakers or jeans.

Cell Phones
At most restaurants, it is considered discourteous to leave your cell phone turned on or to carry on cell phone conversations.

Meal Times
Breakfast is usually served in diners and coffee shops from about 6am to 10am. Lunch is available from about 11:30am to 2pm, dinner from about 5pm to 10pm. Many pubs and restaurants offer a late-night menu. Brunches are often served on weekends only – and at some spots, on Sundays only – usually from 11am to 2pm or later.

Left **Sylvia Hotel** Right **Lobby, Inn at False Creek**

TOP 10 Inexpensive Hotels

1 Sylvia Hotel, Vancouver

The West End's grande dame is a favorite for its relaxed yet sophisticated atmosphere and fabulous location right on English Bay. Some rooms are tiny, but the big draws are the lounge and restaurant overlooking the water. Very pet-friendly hotel. Covered paid parking available. ◈ *1154 Gilford St • Map G2 • 604 681 9321 • www. sylviahotel.com • $$*

2 Oceanside Hotel, Vancouver

Located on a quiet side street near English Bay and Stanley Park, this hotel is a friendly oasis in the heart of the West End. One-bedroom apartments and larger available. Free parking. ◈ *1847 Pendrell St • Map G2 • 604 682 5641 • www.oceanside-hotel.com • $$*

3 Inn at False Creek, Vancouver

Decorated Santa Fe-style, this modern, spotless hotel offers large, well-appointed rooms and executive suites. A knock-out location, steps from downtown and Granville Island. ◈ *1335 Howe St • Map J4 • 604 682 0229 • www.innat falsecreek.com • $$*

4 Sandman Suites on Davie, Vancouver

At this West End high-rise, one-bedroom suites offer kitchens, washer/ dryers, balconies, and sofa beds in the living room. The views of English Bay from many of the rooms are a plus. Underground paid parking available. ◈ *1160 Davie St • Map H4 • 604 681 7263 • www.sandman hotels.com • $$$*

5 Ramada Inn and Suites Downtown, Vancouver

Art Deco touches enhance this downtown hotel. A great spot if you want to be as close to clubs and shops as to most central attractions. Air-conditioned rooms; pets welcomed for a fee. ◈ *1221 Granville St • Map J4 • 604 685 1111 • www.ramada vancouver.com • $$*

6 Greenbrier Hotel, Vancouver

Providing a great Robson Street location, this modest hotel's renovated one-bedroom suites have complete kitchens, with other pluses such as free coffee and free parking thrown in. ◈ *1393 Robson St • Map J3 • 604 683 4558 • www.greenbrier hotel.com • $$*

7 Buchan Hotel, Vancouver

This 1926-vintage, three-story property offers good value for money with its European-style, no-frills accommodation and its location: you'd be hard-pressed to sleep closer to Stanley Park – unless you were actually in it.

The communal lounge with a fireplace is a bonus. ◈ *1906 Haro St • Map H2 • 604 685 5354 • www.buchanhotel.com • $*

8 Best Western Chateau Granville, Vancouver

A frequent choice for out-of-towners with an eye for price and location, this 15-story hotel offers mainly one-bedroom suites, but has some smaller, standard rooms as well. Suites come with microwaves and wireless Internet access. Gated parking available for a fee. ◈ *1100 Granville St • Map J4 • 604 669 7070 • www.chateaugranville. com • $$$*

9 Huntingdon Hotel & Suites, Victoria

This full service hotel offers a range of rooms and suites, including family suites for up to six people. Amenities include a restaurant, sauna, and hot tub, as well as meeting facilities. ◈ *330 Quebec St • Map N4 • 250 381 3456 • www. bellevillepark.com • $*

10 Days Inn Victoria on the Harbour

Located downtown, some rooms here offer views of the picturesque Inner Harbour. All are equipped with kitchenettes. Guests can relax in the outdoor whirlpool and seasonal heated pool (Apr–Oct). ◈ *427 Belleville St • Map N4 • 250 386 451 • www. daysinnvictoria.com • $*

Note: *Unless otherwise stated, all hotels accept credit cards and have private bathrooms and air conditioning*

Price Categories

For a standard, double room per night (with breakfast if included), taxes and extra charges.

$	under $100
$$	$100–150
$$$	$150–200
$$$$	$200–300
$$$$$	over $300

Above **Granville Island Hotel**

🔟 Mid-Priced Hotels

1 Days Inn Vancouver Downtown

Although the heritage building housing this small hotel was built in 1910, the simple but comfortable rooms have been fully renovated. A restaurant and lounge are found onsite, while myriad dining and sightseeing options are within walking distance. 🔖 *921 W Pender St • Map K3 • 604 681 4335 • www.daysinnvancouver. com • $$*

2 Granville Island Hotel, Vancouver

With delightful rooms overlooking False Creek, this intimate hotel, located right on Granville Island, features wooden shutters, beamed ceilings, and oversized bath tubs. Dine at the Dockside restaurant, or choose from the many nearby eateries. 🔖 *1253 Johnston St • Map H5 • 604 683 7373 • www.granvilleisland hotel.com • $$$$*

3 Georgian Court Hotel, Vancouver

Providing a great location for sports fans in town to take in a game – BC Place Stadium and GM Place are mere minutes away – this well-appointed hotel offers air-conditioned rooms, fitness center, and complimentary Internet. Enjoy the two on-site restaurants, including the renowned William Tell. 🔖 *773 Beatty St • Map K4 • 604 682 5555 • www. georgian court.com • $$$*

4 St. Regis Hotel, Vancouver

In an ideal location for shopping and clubbing, the St. Regis offers some rooms with balconies, oversized tubs, and stellar views of the harbor, city, and mountains. All rooms have hi-tech amenities, and free local calls and Internet access. 🔖 *602 Dunsmuir St • Map K3 • 604 681 1135 • www. stregishotel.com • $$$*

5 Residence Inn Vancouver Downtown

Close to Yaletown and the Davie St shopping area, this hotel's spacious suites with kitchens and seating areas make for a great extended stay option. The hotel operates an environmentally conscious "zero waste" program. 🔖 *1234 Hornby St • Map J4 • 604 688 1234 • www.marriott. com • $$$*

6 Blue Horizon Hotel, Vancouver

Gorgeous views abound, as each room in this contemporary hotel has wraparound windows and a balcony. Add to that a fridge, coffee maker, air-conditioning, and more. 🔖 *1225 Robson St • Map J3 • 604 688 1411 • www. bluehorizonhotel.com • $$$*

7 Century Plaza Hotel & Spa, Vancouver

This hotel is a modest, good-value choice. The big draw here is the European-style spa *(see p56)* with indoor pool and steam room. Convenient lounge, restaurant, and cappuccino bar. 🔖 *1015 Burrard St • Map J4 • 604 687 0575 • www.century-plaza.com • $$$*

8 Hotel Grand Pacific, Victoria

Voted Best Hotel in Canada by Condé Nast Traveler Readers' Choice Award. All guest rooms and suites have private balconies, air conditioning, and high-speed Internet access. 🔖 *463 Belleville St • Map N4 • 250 386 0450 • www. hotelgrandpacific.com • $$$*

9 Magnolia Hotel & Spa, Victoria

This award-winning hotel wins over guests with its unbeatable location and service. Rooms feature four-poster beds and marble bathrooms with deep soaker tubs. 🔖 *623 Courtney St • Map P3 • 250 381 0999 • www. magnoliahotel.com • $$$*

10 Chateau Victoria Hotel & Suites, Victoria

Located steps away from Victoria's Inner Harbour, this Four Star Canada Select Hotel with spacious rooms and suites features Victoria's only rooftop restaurant and lounge on the 18th floor. 🔖 *740 Burdett St • Map Q3 • 250 382 4221 • www. chateauvictoria.com • $$$*

Left **Rosewood Hotel Georgia** Right **Bedroom, Opus Hotel Vancouver**

ᴛᴏᴘ10 Luxury & Boutique Hotels

1 Opus Hotel Vancouver

This stylish boutique hotel is a Yaletown trend-setter. Take advantage of the on-site French brasserie and sophisticated lounge to relax after a busy day. ◈ *322 Davie St • Map J5 • 604 642 6787 • www. opushotel.com • $$$$*

2 Westin Bayshore, Vancouver

Sitting on Coal Harbour, between Stanley Park and downtown, this hotel offers guests the best of both worlds: nature and outdoor activities plus the downtown hustle and bustle, with comfortable rooms to retreat to after a busy day. ◈ *1601 Bayshore Drive • Map H2 • 604 682 3377 • www.westin bayshore.com • $$$$*

3 Listel Vancouver Hotel

A beautiful boutique hotel whose rooms are filled with art by top local artists and supplied with literary gems, some by West Coast authors. O'Doul's Restaurant and Bar *(see p74)* provides nightly live music. ◈ *1300 Robson St • Map J3 • 604 684 8461 • www.listel-vancouver. com • $$$$*

4 Shangri-La Hotel, Vancouver

In the heart of Downtown, this hotel offers 119 luxurious rooms. Oversized bathrooms have TVs embedded in

mirrors. Many rooms have balconies, and all are pet-friendly. ◈ *1128 West Georgia St • Map K3 • 604 689 1120 • www.shangri-la. com • $$$$$*

5 Wedgewood Hotel, Vancouver

Owner Eleni Skalbania is as famous as her boutique hotel with its European flair. Caters to those who prefer their accommodation upscale, verging on exclusive. Maid service twice daily says it all. ◈ *845 Hornby St • Map J3 • 604 689 7777 • www.wedgewoodhotel. com • $$$$*

6 Rosewood Hotel Georgia, Vancouver

Treat yourself to a stay at this elegant and legendary retreat. First opened as the Hotel Georgia in 1927, it has been beautifully restored, winning honors on Condé Nast Traveler's Hot List. The spa and restaurant are exemplary. ◈ *801 W Georgia St • Map J3 • 604 682 5566 • www.rosewood hotels.com • $$$$$*

7 Metropolitan Hotel, Vancouver

Everything is done to cosset guests, including European down duvets, marble bathrooms, indoor pool and health club, business center, restaurant, and lounge. An award-winning gem. One smoking floor. ◈ *645 Howe St • Map K3*

• *604 687 1122*
• *www.metropolitan.com*
• *$$$$*

8 Fairmont Empress Hotel, Victoria

The most famous hotel on the West Coast, Victoria's luxury property offers somewhat small but always elegant rooms. Make a reservation to take English-style tea in its glorious lobby *(see p99)*, a pricey but noteworthy experience. ◈ *721 Government St • Map P4 • 250 384 8111 • www.fairmont.com/ empress • $$$$$*

9 Wickaninnish Inn, Long Beach

Perched dramatically on a rocky shelf overlooking Chesterman Beach, this highly acclaimed inn offers luxurious lodgings done in modern West Coast style. With its gorgeous spa and gourmet restaurant, this is the perfect getaway spot *(see pp 32-3)*. ◈ *Osprey Lane, Tofino • Map A4 • 250 725 3100 • www. wick-inn.com • $$$$$*

10 Oak Bay Beach Hotel, Victoria

This historically-rich hotel features waterfront rooms with oversized windows that showcase spectacular ocean views. All rooms offer a gas fireplace and large spa bathrooms. Amenities include seaside spa, fitness center, fine dining, and theater. ◈ *1175 Beach Drive • 250 598 4556 • www.oakbay beachhotel.com • $$$$$*

Note: *Unless otherwise stated, all hotels accept credit cards and have private bathrooms and air conditioning*

Price Categories

For a standard,	**$** under $100
double room per	**$$** $100–150
night (with breakfast	**$$$** $150–200
if included), taxes	**$$$$** $200–300
and extra charges.	**$$$$$** over $300

Above **Pan Pacific Vancouver**

🔟 Business & Suite Hotels

1 Pan Pacific Vancouver

Soaring over the waterfront, the Pan's rooms and luxury suites provide spectacular views of the North Shore mountains. The convention center is in the same complex. Regarded as North America's premiere convention hotel. ⊗ 300-999 Canada Place • Map L2 • 604 662 8111 • http://vancouver.pan pacific.com • $$$$$

2 Coast Plaza Hotel and Suites, Vancouver

Located in the West End, this award-winning hotel offers rooms and suites, 22 meeting rooms, a garden terrace, restaurant, 24-hour room service, and a well-appointed health club. ⊗ 1763 Comox St • Map G2 • 604 688 7711 • www.coasthotels.com • $$$$

3 Delta Vancouver Suite Hotel

An all-suite luxury hotel, centrally located, offering state-of-the-art in-room technology, comfort, and convenience. A restaurant, lounge, and a full health club round out the amenities. ⊗ 550 W Hastings St • Map K3 • 604 689 8188 • www.deltahotels.com • $$$$

4 Fairmont Waterfront, Vancouver

Linked to the convention center by an enclosed walkway, this harborside property is on Condé Nast magazine's gold list. Amenities include Fairmont Gold concierge service, and a year-round outdoor heated pool. Rooms are plush, tranquil. ⊗ 900 Canada Place Way • Map L3 • 604 691 1991 • www.fairmont.com/waterfront-vancouver • $$$$$

5 Four Seasons Hotel, Vancouver

The ideal business location, centrally located above the Pacific Centre Mall, this hotel goes the extra mile, with a 24-hour concierge, health club, indoor/outdoor pool, elegant lounge and restaurant, meeting facilities, 24-hour room service, and valet parking. ⊗ 791 W Georgia St • Map K3 • 604 689 9333 • www.fourseasons.com • $$$$$

6 Lord Stanley Suites on the Park, Vancouver

Furnished one- and two-bedroom suites close to Stanley Park are a good choice for extended stays. Free continental breakfast, underground parking, fitness center, and sauna. ⊗ 1889 Alberni St • Map H2 • 604 688 9299 • www.lordstanley.com • $$$$

7 910 Beach Apartment Hotel, Vancouver

Offers a variety of fully equipped suites, some with goodies such as in-suite washer and dryer. Rates include use of the fitness center and continental breakfast. Underground paid parking. ⊗ 910 Beach Ave • Map H5 • 604 609 5100 • www.910beach.com • $$$

8 Sunset Inn and Suites, Vancouver

Found in the lively West End in a high-rise building, this property's location is nonetheless off the main thoroughfare, so quieter than some. Suitable for short- and long-term stays; rooms come with free high-speed, wireless Internet. ⊗ 1111 Burnaby St • Map H4 • 604 688 2474 • www.sunsetinn.com • $$$

9 Inn at Laurel Point, Victoria

Spacious rooms come with a view of Victoria's Inner Harbour. Sunday buffet-style brunch in the Aura Restaurant is a must. ⊗ 680 Montreal St • 250 386 8721 • www.laurel point.com • $$$$

🔟 Delta Victoria Ocean Pointe Resort and Spa

This renovated Delta hotel is ideally located on the inner harbor and a 5-minute walk to downtown Victoria. Floor-to-ceiling windows in the restaurant offer excellent harbor views. Good value special offers and spa packages. ⊗ 45 Songhees Rd • 250 360 2999 • www.deltahotels.com • $$$

Left **Guestroom, O Canada House** Right **Front porch, West End Guest House**

Bed & Breakfasts

O Canada House, Vancouver

Built in 1897, this delightful guesthouse reflects the early elegance of the West End, including a parlor with a fireplace. King- and queen-bedded rooms with private baths. Gourmet breakfast included. ✪ 1114 Barclay St • Map J3 • 604 688 0555 • www.ocanadahouse.com • $$$$

West End Guest House, Vancouver

A pretty pink and grey 1906 Victorian inn near Stanley Park offering one- and two-bedroom suites. Free parking, bike storage, telephones in rooms. Full hot breakfast served. ✪ 1362 Haro St • Map J3 • 604 681 2889 • www.westendguesthouse.com • $$$

Corkscrew Inn B&B, Vancouver

In a lovely restored 1912 Craftsman-style house, this funky Kitsilano B&B combines Art Deco charm – including dozens of stained-glass windows – with upscale amenities, such as feather beds, robes, and high-speed Internet. Take a peek at the curios in the small wine museum. ✪ 2735 W 2nd Ave • Map B2 • 604 733 7276 • www.corkscrewinn.com • $$$

English Bay Inn, Vancouver

A West End hideaway with cozy antique furniture, queen-sized beds, and ensuite bathrooms. The full breakfast by the fireplace is a pleasant start to the day. Free parking. ✪ 1968 Comox St • Map G2 • 604 683 8002 • www.englishbayinn.com • $$$$

Fairholme Manor, Victoria

This delightfully restored Victorian mansion offers six luxurious suites overlooking the Olympic Mountains and the Juan de Fuca Straight. Breakfasts are delicous, feature local produce, and can be enjoyed on the porch. ✪ 638 Rockland Place • Map J3 • 250 598 3240 • www.fairholmemanor.com • $$$$$

Victorian Hotel, Vancouver

Built in 1898 as one of the city's first guesthouses, this hotel has been carefully restored to retain its Victorian-era ambience, with bay windows, high ceilings, antique furnishings, and hardwood floors. A comfortable setting, with beautiful bathrooms and down duvets on the beds. Secured parking available for a fee. ✪ 514 Homer St • Map L3 • 604 681 6369 • www.victorianhotel.ca • $$

Barclay House B&B, Vancouver

A perennial West End favorite, this classic 1904 home features spacious two-room suites, attentive staff, a full three-course breakfast, champagne on

arrival, in-room portable phones, and more. Free parking. ✪ 1351 Barclay St • Map H3 • 604 605 1351 • www.barclayhouse.com • $$$

Abigail's Hotel, Victoria

A heritage, Tudor-style B&B-inn with English-style gardens. Charming touches, such as country furnishings, fresh flowers, and a gourmet breakfast. Some rooms with whirlpool tubs or wood-burning fireplaces. ✪ 906 McClure St • 250 388 5363 • www.abigailshotel.com • $$$$$

Heathergate House, Victoria

A near-perfect location on Victoria's busy Inner Harbour, yet a quiet environment. The invitingly posh rooms all have private bath. A well-appointed garden cottage easily sleeps four. Full English breakfast included. ✪ 122 Simcoe St • 250 383 0068 • www.heathergatebb.com • $$

Beaconsfield Inn, Victoria

Dark mahogany floors, antiques, fireplaces, featherbeds, and private bathrooms all add to the stately ambience at this award-winning 1905 Victoria heritage manor. Full breakfast, English tea, and daily sherry included. ✪ 998 Humboldt St • 250 384 4044 • www.beaconsfieldinn.com • $$$$

For more bed & breakfasts, visit the website www.bedandbreakfasts-bc.com

Price Categories

For a standard, double room per night with breakfast if included, taxes and extra charges.

$	under $100
$$	$100–150
$$$	$150–200
$$$$	$200–300
$$$$$	over $300

Above **Entrance, YWCA Hotel/Residence**

TOP 10 Budget Accommodation

1 University of British Columbia, Vancouver

From May to August, take your pick of 3,000 rooms on UBC's beautiful campus. Year-round, one-bedroom suites with kitchens are available. UBC is a city in itself, with many amenities on its grounds. ⬙ 5961 Student Union Blvd • Map A2 • 604 822 1000 • www.ubcconferences.com • $

2 YWCA Hotel/Residence, Vancouver

A secure, 12-story high-rise with air-conditioned rooms to suit all travelers, including families. A good location for those who need their gym fix, with free admission to the fitness center. TVs in some rooms. Wheelchair accessible. ⬙ 733 Beatty St • Map L4 • 604 895 5830 • www.ywcahotel.com • $

3 Hostelling International Vancouver Downtown

Shared and private rooms are offered in this friendly West End spot. Free breakfast is served, while the shared kitchen can help with the other meals. Internet access and secure storage lockers. Open 24 hours. ⬙ 1114 Burnaby St • Map H4 • 604 684 4565 • www.hihostels.ca • $

4 Hostelling International Vancouver Central

A modern hostel, with private rooms as well as traditional dormitory rooms. Efficiently run, and located in the heart of Vancouver's nightclub district. A laundry, kitchen, and bar all onsite. ⬙ 1025 Granville St • Map J4 • 604 685 5335 • www.hihostels.ca • $

5 Hostelling International Vancouver Jericho Beach

This hostel is a 30-minute bus ride from downtown and worth the trip. Open 24 hours, this beachside spot features shared and private rooms and a cook-it-yourself, shared kitchen. Secure storage lockers. Closed during the winter season. ⬙ 1515 Discovery St • Map A2 • 604 224 3208 • www.hihostels.ca/vancouverjerichobeach • $

6 Moda Hotel, Vancouver

A boutique hotel in a heritage 1908 building that blends old-world style with contemporary interiors. Rooms feature flat-screen TVs, high-speed Internet access, and coffee machines. Pets are welcome. ⬙ 900 Seymour St • Map K4 • 604 683 4251 • www.modahotel.ca • $$

7 Kingston Hotel, Vancouver

A relaxed, spotless 1910 heritage building with private and shared baths, a TV lounge, day and overnight storage, sauna, and restaurant. Free continental breakfast. ⬙ 757 Richards St • Map K4 • 604 684 9024 • www.kingstonhotelvancouver.com • $$

8 C & N Backpackers Hostel, Vancouver

In a just-off-central location, with transit and bus depot nearby, is this friendly hostel with shared kitchens and Internet access. Clean, private, and shared non-smoking rooms, with single-sex dorms. Some rooms with TV. ⬙ 927 Main St • 604 682 2441 • www.cnnbackpackers.com • $

9 Ocean Island Backpackers Inn, Victoria

Clean, comfortable and funky, the site is a secure historic building near Victoria's Inner Harbour. Dorms and private rooms with 24-hour check-in. ⬙ 791 Pandora Ave • Map Q2 • 250 385 1788/9 • www.oceanisland.com • $

10 Paul's Motor Inn, Victoria

Centrally located in a safe area, Paul's is a clean, comfortable base from which to enjoy Victoria's activities, sights, restaurants, and shops. All rooms have mini fridges, TVs, and Internet access. ⬙ 1900 Douglas St • Map Q2 • 250 382 9231 • www.paulsmotorinn.com • $

Some accomodations, especially those in private homes or heritage buildings, are not wheelchair accessible. Check before booking.

General Index

Acknowledgments

The Author

Long time BC resident Constance Brissenden lives in downtown Vancouver. She has written numerous travel, history, and children's books, and is co-author of the Dorling Kindersley *Eyewitness Travel Guide to the Pacific Northwest.*

Produced by International Book Productions Inc., Toronto

Editorial Director Barbara Hopkinson
Art Editor James David Ellis
Editors Judy Phillips, Sheila Hall, Quadrum Solutions
Senior DTP Designer Dietmar Kokemohr
Photo Research and Permissions Sheila Hall
Proofreader Helen Townsend
Indexer Barbara Sale Schon
Photographer Cylla von Tiedemann
Additional Photography Tim Draper

AT DORLING KINDERSLEY
Senior Editor Kathryn Lane
Art Editor Shahid Mahmood
Publishing Managers Jane Ewart, Scarlett O'Hara
Publisher Douglas Amrine
Designer Gadi Farfour
Revisions Team
Emma Anacootee, Marta Bescos, Nadia Bonomally, Rhiannon Furbear, Rose Hudson, Laura Jones, Priya Kukadia, Jude Ledger, Hayley Maher, Nicola Malone, Jane Mundy, Marisa Renzullo, Stuti Tiwari, Nikhil Verma, Joe Wiebe
Senior Cartographic Editor Casper Morris
Senior DTP Designer Jason Little
Production Louise Daly

Maps Mapping Ideas Ltd.
DK Picture Library
Romaine Werblow

Picture Credits
a-above; b-below/bottom; c-centre; f-far; l-left; r-right; t-top.

The publishers would like to thank the following individuals, companies, and picture libraries for their kind permission to reproduce their photographs:

ALCAN DRAGON BOAT FESTIVAL: Jessica Bushey 44c

BARD ON THE BEACH SHAKESPEARE FESTIVAL staging of Much Ado About Nothing (2004): 44tl; JON BENJAMIN: 13TR, 13CL; BC PLACE: 42tr; BILL REID FOUNDATION: Kenji Nagai 35tr; BLUE WATER CAFE: 40br; BUTCHART GARDENS LTD, Victoria, BC, Canada: 38tl, 101tr

CANADA PLACE CORPORATION: 4–5, CAPILANO SUSPENSION BRIDGE PARK: 6clb, 14crb, 14–15c, 15tc, 15bl, 46br; CHILL WINSTON: 64tr; CIRCLE CRAFT CO-OP: hand blown glass cups by Miyuki Shinkai 81tl; CITY OF VANCOUVER ARCHIVES: 11cr, 31cra; CITY OF VANCOUVER: *Inukshuk* by Alvin Kanak 1986 8tl, *The Crab* by George Norris 1968 34br, *Captain John Deighton (Gassy Jack)* by Vern Simpson 1970 60cra, *Gate to the Northwest Pas-sage* by Alan Chung Hung 1980 76tl; COAST RESTAURANT: 73tl; CYPRESS MOUNTAIN: 48tr

DANIEL LE CHOCOLAT BELGE: 72tr;

EDIBLE CANADA: 21cr;

FAIRMONT HOTELS & RESORTS: 30tl, 64tr, 69tr, 92–3; FOUR SEASONS RESORT WHISTLER: Michael Rafelson 29tl, 57tl

GALLERY CAFE & CATERING: 75tl; GROUSE MOUNTAIN RESORT: 3tr; HARBOUR CENTRE/THE LOOKOUT!: 61b, 66–7; HAWKSWORTH RESTAURANT: 40tl; HSBC CELEBRATION OF LIGHT: 44bl

INN AT FALSE CREEK: 114tr; THE IRISH HEATHER: 51tr METROPOLITAN HOTELS: 41t; MUNRO'S BOOKS: 98tr; MUSEUM OF ANTHROPOLOGY AT UBC: The Raven and the First Men by Bill Reid 1980 34ca, 36tl

THE NEW OXFORD: 82tr; NEW-SMALL & STERLING, LTD: 54cb

OPUS HOTEL: 116tr

PACIFIC PALISADES HOTEL: 113tl; THE POURHOUSE: 65tl; PRINCE OF WHALES WHALE WATCHING: 100tl

RAILWAY CLUB: 74tl; ROSEWOOD HOTEL GEORGIA: 116tl; ROYAL BRITISH COLUMBIA MUSEUM: 7cla, ,24cb, 24cla, 24-25c, 25tl, 25cr, 96tr

SCIENCE WORLD BC: 23tl; SIMPSON PUBLIC RELATIONS: John Sherlock Studios 82tl; SQUAMISH CHAMBER OF COMMERCE/www.squamish.ca: Garry Broeckling 87cl; Todd Lawson 49sb, 89tl; Bill McComish 39sb, 89tr

TOP TABLE RESTAURANT GROUP: 90tl; TOURISM VANCOUVER ISLAND: 26–7c

UNIVERSITY OF BRITISH COLUMBIA MUSEUM OF ANTHROPOLOGY: Bill McLennan 6bl, 16bc, 16cl, 16tr, 16–17; The Raven and the First Men Bill Reid 17bl; VANCOUVER AQUARIUM: 10tr, 10tl, 10c, 11bl, 46tr; VANCOUVER ART GALLERY: Emily Carr, Logger's Culls, 1935, oil on canvas, Collection of the Vancouver Art Gallery, Gift of Miss I. Parkyn, VAG 39.1, Photo: Trevor Mills

18–19c; Robert Davidson, Eagles, 1991, gouache and watercolour on paper, Vancouver Art Gallery Acquisi-tion Fund, VAG 94.3, Photo: Teresa Healy; 19bl; Ken Lum, Four Boats Stranded: Red and Yellow, Black and White, 2000, polyurethane, steel, fiberglass, and paint, Vancouver Art Gallery Major Purchase Fund, the Canada Millennium Bureau and the BC 2000 Community Spirit Fund; VAG 2000.25 a-d, Photo:Colin Goldie 18bc; 18cla; VANCOUVER CIVIC THEATRES: 42tl, 43tr; VANCOUVER FANCLUB: Ron Sombilon 50tr; VANCOUVER MUSEUM, CANADA (QFA 233): 76tr; VANCOUVER SYMPHONY ORCHESTRA: 45sb; VIDA WELLNESS SPAS: 56tl

WILDEBEEST: Andrew Morrison 40tr; WHISTLER BLACKCOMB RESORT: Therese Lundgren 3br, Insight Photography 7crb, Toshi Kawano 28–9c, 30tl; WICKANINNISH INN: 32–3; THE WOOD CO-OP GALLERY: 21bc

YVR ART FEDERATION: The Spirit of Haida Gwaii: The Jade Canoe by Bill Reid 1994, Photo: Bill MacLennan 34c; Coast Salish Welcome Figures by Susan Point 1996, Photo: Kenji Nagai 37bl

All other images are © Dorling Kindersley. For further information see www.dkimages.com

Special Editions of DK Travel Guides

DK Travel Guides can be purchased in bulk quantities at discounted prices for use in promotions or as premiums. We are also able to offer special editions and personalized jackets, corporate imprints, and excerpts from all of our books, tailored specifically to meet your own needs.

To find out more, please contact:

(in the United States)
SpecialSales@dk.com

(in the UK)
travelspecialsales@uk.dk.com

(in Canada) DK Special Sales at
general@tourmaline.ca

(in Australia) **business.development@pearson.com.au**

Selected Street Index